The American Way
Why Superman© Got it Wrong
The Complete Collection

Thomas Purcell

Copyright © 2012 edition Thomas Purcell

ISBN-13: 978-1463696603

ISBN: 1463696604

DEDICATION

This book is dedicated to the Clan of the Black Lotus, a worldwide gaming club, and some of the best friends an author could have

Also

To the bunny wherever they might be sleeping tonight

ACKNOWLEDGMENTS

I'd like to make mention of the following people who have helped, guided, inspired, angered or otherwise influenced me in the creation of this book—for better or worse

(in no particular order)

Jim Sharpe, John McJunkin, Mike Broomhead and the crew at 550 KFYI AM

Feminists, The OWS Movement and other leftist malcontents

Alan Colmes

Sean Hannity

Barack Obama

Glen Beck

The American Tea Party

And

Too many others to list.

CONTENTS

Thomas Purcell

1 AUTHOR'S INTRODUCTION

In the long history of the world, only a few generations have been granted the role of defending freedom in its hour of maximum danger. I do not shrink from this responsibility—I welcome it.- John F Kennedy

Recently there have been stories in the news about the upcoming issue of Superman #900, where Superman declares himself a citizen of the world and revokes his own American citizenship due to an incident involving Iranian protests. According to Comics Alliance:

...In it, Superman consults with the President's national security advisor, who is incensed that Superman appeared in Tehran to non-violently support the protesters demonstrating against the Iranian regime, no doubt an analogue for the recent real-life protests in the Middle East. However, since Superman is viewed as an American icon in the DC Universe as well as our own, the Iranian government has construed his actions as the will of the American President, and indeed, an act of war. Superman replies that it was foolish to think that his actions would not reflect politically on the American government, and that he therefore plans to renounce his American citizenship at the United Nations the next day -- and

to continue working as a superhero from a more global than national perspective- (Comics Alliance, 2011.)

Well Superman, you got it wrong. Although in the comic book his actions may have been interpreted as an act of war, there are some things that are worth fighting for, and yes, worth dying for. Freedom is one of those things, as is the right of a single human being to express himself free of tyranny. Tyranny often takes on many different colors and waves many flags--some of them even carry the banners of democracy. More countries today are democracies than ever before, yet the disparity of wealth and the oppressive nature of countries and governments has not changed substantially since the 1700's. If more countries are supposedly free democracies, this asks a paradoxical question: Is it merely democracy that allows Americans to prosper? Or is it our Constitution? Or the American people themselves?

In 1776 a group of stalwart farmers, lawyers and town leaders formed a governmental committee and wrote a document that has stood the test of time. This group, called the First Constitutional Congress, declared that American colonies were to be independent of their mother country England. They declared the King's will invalid within the borders of America, and they would no longer obey English Law or the decrees of the crown of England. This document came to be known as the Declaration of Independence and following the signing of that document, it took these 13 colonies more than 10 years of war and strife to finally form the first true representative democracy in human history—the United States of America.

Since that time, although many nations have been formed as democracies, the United States stands unique. To date it is the only government that has as its forming a documented list of rights of the people as endowed to them by their creator limiting government rather than government being the arbiter of rights and limits placed up its people.

Over the next 200 plus years both England and its fellow European countries have gradually moved toward a more representative government themselves. They now have various forms of the democratic process such as free elections, and in most cases they have deposed the monarchies that originally governed them. But in that time they have not achieved the level of individual freedom that America had in its infancy. In fact, America has moved further back toward this European style of government where people rely on the state for their immediate needs and support. In this sense, while Europe has become more free, America has become less, and the socialization of its societal systems has grown almost as large as Europe's.

In the American media, and in its white marbled halls of government, there is a call to become even more like Europe and other more restrictive governments. It is said that Europe has a more meaningful set of protections in place for its elderly, sick and disabled. The progressive forces and the Democratic party are attempting to move America in that direction to gain those protections for the American people. Yet there is a great deal of resistance from Americans on some if not all of these issues. A segment of America views the move toward increased social structuring and modeling our society after the European social constructs as counterproductive and antithetical to American life.

A strict interpretation of the American Constitution (1787) argues in their favor. Those that support change toward socialization point out that the Constitution was intended to be a flexible document. While the Constitution was meant to be amended and adjusted by the changing needs of a growing nation, its rules and rights certainly could not, and should not, be called flexible. The very inflexibility of both the document, and the rights it spells out, are inherent in all men and contributes to its unique status.

This is key to the Constitution and the "American Way"-- that our rights come not from government or law, but are from God, or inherent in all men by nature. The average American citizen often talks about the American way of life but rarely can elucidate on the exact specifics of what makes America unique. There are the usual references to hot dogs, baseball, fast cars and freedom, but a concrete assessment as to what defines America often escapes the average citizen. This book seeks to correct that and give the reader a true understanding of the foundations of freedom and the defining events that helped to build the United States and the mystique of the "American Way."

This unique status, and the country that it is built upon, the United States, is under constant attack and criticism by those who do not live under its law or often by those that have benefitted the most from its freedoms. To understand why the United States is the beacon of the world, or should be, is something these critics cannot seem to fathom nor do they understand why America has reached the zenith of human success. They, like the people that defend the "American Way," also have no true understanding of the reasons for America's greatness. This book is for them as well; to perhaps re-educate the devalued mind of the liberal who has begun to question the failed leadership of current President, Barack Obama, and ask themselves if his leadership, or indeed the leadership of leftist thinking, is improving the life of the average American or hindering it.

This is why Superman is so very wrong. To understand what America stands for, it sometimes has to be defended no matter who might be offended, insulted, or driven to violence, such as in the Iranian situation described in the comic book (issue #900.) Superman does not want to impose an American value system upon them, and wanted to act freely without political consequences for America. But that would be a fatal error for the character and this book explains why—it explains why America is not flawed for attempting to spread its ideals and why the consequences of such actions and the price paid for it is one that Americans have not only been historically willing to pay, but has paid big dividends in the long run.

The American Way: Why Superman Got It Wrong, is designed to address that misunderstanding and to explain to America's detractors what it is that is the source of our success--the American way of life, its Constitution and the principles of self- determination, self-sacrifice, and our single minded focus on placing the individual superior to the group and holding the individual accountable and responsible for his actions.

It has been our departure from that focus that has weakened America over the past 40 years, and we must return to it to maintain our place in the world. The derivation of freedom and liberty do not end at our borders, but are in fact, exportable ideas that should be promoted and given to other cultures as a source of inspiration. The grand strategy of America's enemies is to do that very thing, spread their own anti-American ideas in order to foment distrust, fear and outright hated of America and its freedoms.

Superman should have known this--because any farm boy raised in Smallville, Kansas would have even if Kal-El the Kryptonian did not.

2 GOD PLANTS A MAYFLOWER

Thus out of small beginnings greater things have been produced by His hand that made all things of nothing, and gives being to all things that are; and, as one small candle may light a thousand, so the light here kindled hath shown unto many, yea in some sort to our whole nation; let the glorious name of Jehovah have all the praise.- William Bradford, 1630

In the years following the success of the Jamestown colony, the first permanent English settlement in the New World, settlers from European nations began to flow to the shores of America with a unique sense of purpose. Although the hardships of life in the new found lands of the Americas were well documented among the early potential settlers, the legends of great potential riches also walked hand in hand with the stories of the horrors. Starvation, hostile natives and harsh weather conditions were brushed aside with the potential for great riches. Used potential too many times. Do a rewrite.

Despite the modern day historian's view of the early settlers motives, the primary reason so many settlers came to the New World was not the untold wealth of resources and land that America offered. The first major expansion of the New World settlements was a small group of what could best be called religious malcontents, the Pilgrims.[1] While wealth was a possibility, the primary reason most of the passengers of the Mayflower made the voyage was an escape from the perception that England had become an oppressive government--certainly religiously oppressive.

The Pilgrims were religious separatists, and by some accounts, political zealots as well.[2] They had little in common with a government that was run by the King of England who was less than open minded about the Pilgrims' view of God and religion. In England the primary religion and the Crown were one and the same--the Church of England. Laws were in place that required everyone to attend the same church services and declared the King and the of the church as one in the same. The Pilgrims and their Separatist Faith, according to the Columbia Encyclopedia,[3] stated that,

"Although not actively persecuted, the group was subjected to ecclesiastical investigation and to the mockery, criticism, and disfavor of their neighbors."

---

[1] any of the English Puritans who founded Plymouth Colony in Massachusetts in 1620

[2] H.L. Mencken- "Puritanism: The haunting fear that someone, somewhere, may be happy", from *A Book of Burlesques* (1916)

[3] The Columbia Encyclopedia. "Pilgrims" 2008.

Hardly an environment to practice their own faith, let alone get ahead in society either professionally or financially.

According to Bradford's[4] own journals of the Mayflower voyage, which is the only known account other than personal letters, more than half of the Mayflower's passengers were fleeing religious tyranny and persecution. While many of the craftsmen and others who came along for the voyage were along for other reasons, such as wealth or prosperity, they were chiefly indentured servants to the company they contracted with for the trip, and if not entirely enamored of the Separatists, they certainly were more tolerant of their religion than the society they were leaving.

"Leaving" as an understatement for the lifetime commitment they were making. The journey to the New World was more than perilous; it was downright deadly with many of the passengers dying en route to the New World. Barely over half of the total passengers and crew survived the voyage to the New World, facing scurvy, storms and dysentery on the trip.[5] The surviving members of the passengers and crew certainly were the most determined and hardy of the group, a fact that is often overlooked in the

---

[4] Written between 1630 and 1647 the journal describes the story of the Pilgrims from 1608, when they settled in Holland, through the 1620 *Mayflower* voyage, until the year 1647. The book ends with a list, written in 1650, of *Mayflower* passengers.

[5] On the morning of November 9, after more than two months at sea (not to mention a month of delays on board the ships back in England) they spotted land, which they later found to be Cape Cod. After 2750 miles, traveling at an average speed of just under two mph, the voyage was over. Of the 102 original passengers, manifests indicate less than 60 survivors among the ship and crew.

historical context of the importance of the Plymouth colony and the relevance of the Mayflower voyage. By some accounts 18% of today's population of New England can trace their roots back to that group of Mayflower survivors.[6] To this day, the residents of Maine, Massachusetts, New Hampshire and surrounding states make it a point of pride to be typically more independent minded and stalwart than their American cousins across the country. The state motto of New Hampshire is "Live Free or Die." The ideals of the Plymouth colonists live on in the bloodlines of today's New Englander. Although the New England area is decidedly liberal in its political leanings by the dint of strict vote count and voter registration records, the individual New Englander will be happy to recount tales of their tough and independent nature and lifestyle.[7]

To emphasize how difficult the voyage must have been, the colonists, upon arriving on the shores of what is now known as Cape Cod, Massachusetts, were in virtual rebellion with the captain and crew of the Mayflower because they had arranged to be delivered to the more hospitable climate of Virginia. As a result, to maintain order and establish some sort of peaceful basis upon which to build the colony, the group established a document that is as unique to the American

---

[6] The General Society of Mayflower Descendants designed a genetic roadmap used to establish and document the lineage based on a summary provided by an unknown ancestor. While it contains some errors (particularly the details of Jonathan Watrous' Revolutionary War service) it has been remarkably accurate and did lead to validation of the lineage.

[7] "Tough New Englanders" Blog by Chris Gregoire, January 2011

school of thought as the Constitution. It was called the Mayflower Compact.

The Mayflower Compact was a document to reestablish the purpose of the colonists and the workers they had contracted to build their colony. Since the original landing was intended to be in Virginia, and the potential wealth and ease of building a colony easier as a result, the group felt it necessary to rewrite their own laws and rules of governance. They recognized the need to rebuild their relationship in view of the catastrophic losses of the voyage and failure of the captain to deliver them to their arranged location in Virginia.

Unfortunately, no known original copy of the Mayflower Compact survived, although Bradford's 1647 journal does have a copied version of the original. While the fundamental argument of the compact is very basic, it stands apart in one important feature--something the colonists probably did not even understand the significance of at the time. According to Bradford's journal, the Compact reads:

Having undertaken, for the Glory of God, and advancements of the Christian faith and honor of our King and Country, a voyage to plant the first colony in the Northern parts of Virginia, do by these presents [sic], solemnly and mutually, in the presence of God, and one another, covenant and combine ourselves together into a civil body politic; for our better ordering, and preservation and furtherance of the ends aforesaid; and by virtue hereof to enact, constitute, and frame, such just and equal laws, ordinances, acts, constitutions, and offices, from time to time, as shall be thought most meet and convenient for the general good of the colony; unto which we promise all due submission and obedience.- (The Mayflower Compact, November 11, 1620)

Note the use of the expression of "just and equal laws"-- not laws as established by then King James. This is a critical distinction that was unique in colonial documents of the period. Up until the Mayflower Compact, most colonial arrangements, such as in the Jamestown Colony, established themselves as essentially extensions of English government and the Crown of England. Although the document makes several references to King James and his sovereignty over the colony, the document clearly establishes the Plymouth colony as equal and separate from England. This was most likely due to the fact that the Pilgrims were not lawyers but religious zealots, and indeed viewed themselves as "separate but equal" which became a central legal precedent in American law. Yet when looking at it from an historical point of view, it is clear that the colonists of Plymouth saw themselves as substantially different from their English brethren. This would be a theme that is carried into American political thought throughout its history and is the kernel of independence that blossomed into the great tree of American political thought today. Another unique and crucial phrase used in the Mayflower Compact refers to King James as the "dread sovereign." In the context used in the document, this term was used in reference to the King as powerful and in reverence--but not in fear as previous documents had used terms in describing the English throne. Once again the Pilgrims were Separatists that were threading the needle of polite reference with the threads of independence that are woven now so intricately into the fabric of the American spirit.

Survival in the Plymouth colony was brutal and relied mostly on the willingness of those early settlers to work until they dropped from exhaustion and live on food that would make a Billy goat wretch. They had brought supplies to last only a few months. They were forced to either farm enough land to live on what they could grow or gather what they could from the native flora and fauna. The stories of the first Thanksgiving that most children read in grade school are hardly accurate insofar as they neglect to mention the ridiculous hardships of the early Pilgrims. While depictions of the local natives in most school books is that of friendly natives bearing gifts of food and comfort; in reality most of the natives were quite hostile to the Pilgrim intruders. While some speak of the relationship between the local natives and the colonists as friendly, the truth is somewhat more checkered.

This is not to say that the early Pilgrims were innocent victims of native hostility. They most certainly were perpetrators of what would be considered by today as crimes of theft and desecration of lands, but you cannot apply the laws and standards of today to the standards and morays of those harsh days. Had the Pilgrims decided to use traditional rules and morays and not raided local lands and burial mounds for stores of corn and food, it is likely the early colony would not have survived, and the remainder of the colony would have been decimated by starvation and exposure. Faced with the prospect of annihilation, it is likely that even today a group of individuals would act similarly.

However, several accounts indicate that while local native stores were raided for food to prevent starvation, they only took what was needed and did not attack or otherwise harm native settlements.[8] The local natives were later on reimbursed for the corn and food supplies that were taken from the stores, as the colony finally established itself with its own crops. Most post-modern accounts of vile actions against the natives are greatly exaggerated and fail to mention this important fact. The Wampanoag Indians, who were the benefactors of this reimbursement which occurred six months after the initial thefts, established strong relations with the Plymouth colonists teaching them more advanced techniques of fishing and farming that would allow the colonists to become less reliant on native handouts. While Miles Standish's aggressive attempt to protect the colony were certainly violent in many cases, his actions revolved around colonial survival, the lack of ability of any retreat back to England, or retreat into the sea. It was not a matter of racial intolerance, religious fervor, or an inherently violent nature of supposedly civilized men. It was a matter of survival.

In fact the local Wampanoag were mostly wiped out by plague and disease probably brought over by the settlers

8 The definitive text on the actions of the early Pilgrims is Mayflower: A Story of Courage, Community, and War. By Nathaniel Philbrick. Illustrated. 461 pp. Viking.

inadvertently. The native people's did not have resistances to diseases that were now commonplace in England and one could hardly blame the first settlers for a process that was out of their control and could hardly understand in modern terms. By the time of King Phillips War, sometimes called the First Indian War, Metacom's War, Metacomet's War, or Metacom's Rebellion the Wampanoag population was now less than 1,000 natives. It was an armed conflict between Native American inhabitants of present-day New England and English colonists and their Native American allies in 1675–78. The war is named after the main leader of the Native American side, Metacomet, known to the English as "King Philip". King Phillip initiated hostilities as colonists encroached on native lands, and was hung for his efforts which led to a furthering of hostilities for years to come. But at the time of the Plymouth colony, the local was both healthy, well off and friendly to the settlers. Free and independent people who engage in trade often thrive, whereas those that become dependent and reliant upon others often fail.

This rebuilding of the colonists' skill sets is a lesson that can translate well to modern political thought and is the basis for the prominent value that American culture over the years has placed on self-reliance. Modern leftist political thought is predicated upon the fact that social structures and societal constructs are necessary to lift individuals out of poverty. This is the reverse of the lessons of the Plymouth colony which learned to be self-reliant on the skill sets they learned. While the benefactors of the Wampanoag's gifts and skill with the native lands, they received such aid only after they had established themselves as a self-sufficient colony and a military threat; after which they learned to continue that self-reliance and grow the colony. They did not come to rely on the natives for their food and comforts except after an initial phase of a choice of starvation or action. Indeed, whatever comforts they had come from their own two hands and they learned to become reliant on their own fortitude and self-sufficiency. Bradford's account of the colony's determined effort to become self-sufficient is well documented in his narrative *Of Plymouth Plantation* (1606).

In his book, mislabeled again by modern day historians as a "journal," Bradford parallels the creation and development of the Plymouth colony closely with that of the Bible with his own religious fervor steeped in its pages. He was patently convinced that the Plymouth colony was deigned to be from divine inspiration and would be the foundation upon which a great nation would be built. He correctly believed the establishment of the Plymouth colony was far more than simply an extension of English lands in America but rather a point of historical and religious significance--one that would ring throughout the ages. Bradford knew full well his own book would play an important role in the understanding of the events of the founding of Plymouth and its historical significance. He writes in chapter six:

I have been the larger in these things, and so shall crave leave in some like passages following, (though in other things I shall labour to be more contract) that their children may see with what difficulties their fathers wrestled in going through these things in their first beginnings, and how God brought them along notwithstanding all their weaknesses and infirmities. As also that some use may be made hereof in after times by others in such like weighty employments; and herewith I will end this chapter.- William Bradford (1606)

It is clear in reading this passage, not only was Bradford aware of the importance of the Plymouth colony but also of his own role in being its governor and sole documentarian of the events. It is a rare individual that has the self-awareness to not only document important events but his own importance in them. Furthermore, Bradford's accounts are clear and free of personal misrepresentation of his own failings--remarkable considering the depth of his religious fervor. Bradford understood with great clarity that without the enormity of the suffering of the entire experience of founding the colony, it is unlikely they would have experienced the joys of freedom and liberty. He writes:

Some times by bloody death and cruell torments; other whiles imprisonments, banishments, and other hard usages; as being loath his kingdom should goe downe, the trueth prevaile, and the churches of God reverte to their anciente puritie, and recover their primative order, libertie, and bewtie. (1607)

In the years that followed, Bradford's original book(s) had fallen into the hands of the Crown of England, possibly taken during the Revolutionary War, but even the English crown understood the importance of the document relative to American political thought and ordered its return to the United States in 1897. Had the book been lost it is unlikely Americans today would have appreciated the unusual events that had transpired in the Plymouth colony that made it unique in political thought and in the American concepts of self-sufficiency and self-reliance. Key to understanding Bradford's state of mind at the writing of his book, was not a focus on his religious fervor, but that of the understanding of the colony's importance insofar as its historical importance.

Bradford has a unique insight into the future of America and what the role of the first colonists would be to the future of an American continent populated by the English and other European powers. Few today could lay claim to such insight in their own future. Indeed, most can only see a few years into their own making. For instance the argument for such edicts as the Patriot Act invariably revolve around "but our President would never use such power against its own citizenry". In fact, one can never know the future and must always assume the worse and thus prepare for it. A man like Bradford saw the potential for great evil in a society that was either godless or one that where the central authority was church based. Instead, the Compact was built and predicated upon the individual and individual rights.

The relationship of the Plymouth colonists to the later schools of American political thought that led to the American Constitution cannot be underestimated. Whereas the Mayflower Compact was the first time English colonists had established a legal framework for independent governance, it was the self-sufficiency of the Plymouth colonists that established the preeminent concepts of self-reliance and self-determination. Without the great suffering and consequence of the Plymouth colonists, the greatness of the later colonies most likely would not have been achieved.

Self-determination was also a crucial factor in the future development of American politics. The Plymouth colonists, either by choice or fate, were now essentially isolated from their English motherland, and they felt they had no legal bond to their original intention. Perhaps it was intended as a statement of religious fervor or merely an act of a careless captain, but the colonists were now forced by their predicament to rely only upon each other for sustenance and safety. Like men trapped in a foxhole with an untenable enemy, the colonists became more reliant upon their own skills and fortitude--probably more than they had originally bargained for.

The Pilgrims were devoutly religious and had lost most of their cultural identity in England. It is no wonder that the life of self-reliance and self-sufficiency suited them well. While the core beliefs of religious freedom were incorporated into later American documents and schools of thought, their self-reliance and self-sufficiency has played just as large a role in American political thought. The Mayflower Compact, while clearly written by deeply religious authors, had in its roots not so much a religious document but a political one. Its base theory of independent governance by consensus rather than monarchical rule is essentially the first known modern document of democratic rule, a fact often overlooked.

Furthermore, the Pilgrims did not see themselves as especially politically motivated nor that much different religiously from their English cousins or roots—merely a difference of opinion of custom and orthodoxy. Yet they were keenly self-aware that once the colony had been founded and the Compact written it was a document of great historical import. Such separation of religious fervor from political governance resounded later on in the American Constitution in its separation of church and state.

The current Constitution clearly states that there will be no establishment of a state religion:

Congress shall make no law respecting an establishment of religion, or prohibiting the free exercise thereof; or abridging the freedom of speech, or of the press; or the right of the people peaceably to assemble, and to petition the Government for a redress of grievances.

That second part of the First Amendment is critical and relates directly back to the Mayflower Compact and the first colonies—the prohibition of the free exercise of religion, and is in fact, a double edged sword to those that would entreat people to ignore our religious heritage. The outright banning of public funding for anything of religious significance or morality was not what was intended in the First, it was designed to prevent such bans or the *establishment* of a state religion. While many may argue that the state should be godless, it's people certainly aren't and therefore government should be a reflection of that—at least this was the intent of Constitutional authors who patterned it after the Mayflower Compact.

The principle colonists of the Plymouth colony and their children were certainly religious--almost to the point of zealotry. Bearing this in mind, there can be no doubt that a fundamental principle of the Constitution was to make sure that as the United States grew, they did not want to fall into the trap that the Plymouth colonists were fleeing from-- namely an official or state religion. The separation of church and state, while clear in the Constitution, does not necessarily mean that America is a godless society. Far from it, without the religious zealotry of Bradford and his fellow Plymouth colonists, they would not have had the stomach to break philosophically and politically from England.

But the Plymouth colonists clearly saw the importance of God and religion in their lives as well as in how they carried out their day to day lives. It is no secret that the Bible teaches the importance of self-reliance.[9] Many passages in the Bible refer to God and the strength of the individual to bear through the trial and tribulations of everyday life without complaint and with forbearance. This basic understanding of

---

[9] Every day we must choose who we will rely on. We can rely on ourselves; we can rely on others; or we can rely on God. It's a question of living by faith or living by sight. We live by sight when we rely on anyone other than God—and we also grow disappointed when they/we let us down. We live by faith when we rely on God—and we never grow disappointed because He is always faithful. When faced with an obstacle or problem, is your first instinct to figure it out and tackle it on your own? Do you immediately think of others you can recruit to help you? Or do you run to God with issue and entrust the dilemma to Him? Relying on ourselves and others is natural; relying on God is supernatural.—*God is king of Self Reliance*, Jeff Miller

the role of God and religion was essential to the survival of the Plymouth colony. While the Pilgrims and their forbears that wrote the Constitution did not want an oppressive state religion, they clearly also did not want a godless society or one that refused to recognize the importance of religion and God in everyday life. The notion of our government today being bereft of all religious symbolism or reference was not the intention of either the Pilgrims or their descendants that wrote our Constitution. A separation of church and state was intended but only insofar as there would be no state sponsored religion nor President that also headed an American Church—if there were such a thing. The confusion between a godless government and one that is tolerant was never intended.

This is a central argument to liberal concept of today's Constitution, that the document is an act of man and therefore flawed and flexible. The leftist believes that the Constitution is a relic from the past and therefore is of limited value and validity. They see a separation of Church and state not as the Plymouth colonists did; as a protection against a king declaring himself as a head of church and state one in the same. Liberals see government instead as a 'godless' state, one that puts no merit in religious merit or background. As such then, the state is in effect its own God and beyond question or redemption for that matter. It is a mindless beast subject to the whims of popular demand. This is not the principles of the Founding Fathers who derived their ideals from their Mayflower forbears who saw religion and being mindful of God as the foundation for an orderly society.

As word of the Plymouth colony's success reached the shores of England and other European powers, people looking to expand their minds, their wealth and those looking for new opportunities soon filled the merchant ships heading westward. The English crown looked the other way on the notions of a free and independent minded colony as long as the shipments of raw materials kept flowing back to Europe because the Pilgrims, and the now growing colonies, were still essentially English citizens. Not seeing the potential dangers to their own authority and too busy counting the gold, the kings and queens of Europe soon turned to warring with each other over the wealth flowing in, leaving the fledgling colonists exactly what they wanted in the first place--freedom and the ability to govern themselves in an economy that was based largely on unfettered capitalism and the promise of protection under a single concept: that all men were equal under the eyes of God, and by default, its government.

Thomas Purcell

3 FREE ECONOMICS FOR A FREE SOCIETY

Legislation can neither be wise nor just which seeks the welfare of a single interest at the expense and to the injury of many and varied interests.- Andrew Johnson

As America progressed from its early colony stages to an established nation, it first had to go through a "blooding" process which all true nations must survive. As explained in chapter one, *God Plants A Mayflower*, it was the very fact that the Plymouth colony had such violent and difficult beginnings that led to its eventual success.

A nation is defined by three things, its borders, its language and its laws. The founding principles of the Mayflower Compact were merely embryonic principles of law in the early 1700's, to say nothing of America's borders and language which were constantly in a nebulous state. Borders were merely guidelines established by the English crown and determined by surveyors who in many times were corrupt or hired by colonial viceroys to settle minor legal quarrels between the individual colonies.

The difference between America's "blooding" phase and that of most other nations is that America built its cities and borders not based on the legal land surveys of collapsed previous governments, such as Europe did after the fall of the Roman Empire, but on essentially open land where no established nation existed. The lands west of the initial founding colonies were virtually bereft of legal deeds and although Native Americans were the indigenous people, they were scattered and essentially a nomadic culture. There were no cities, no roads and certainly no centralized authority.

European nations were much different. Their legal code was much older and developed as the natural progression of failed governments went through periods of enforcement and ebbing of power. Cities in Europe are virtually built on top of one another, rather than as expansions of a smaller colony or city as they are in America. Thus their legal code was the same--built on the ruins of dying cultures rather than through an evolutionary process of creation and revision.

The American legal dynamics were as virginal as its lands and so they evolved into very simple legal practices. Most of the time the law was simply referred back to the Constitution and written based on immediate need rather than legal precedent, at least in the early years. The legal books of 1877 varied little from those of 1777 and were substantially simpler than European code books of that period.

The concept of colonial law was a very simple one that revolved around a limited government to enforce its laws so naturally its penalties and jurisdiction was necessarily simple as well. The concept of an American "bureaucracy" in 1787 was almost unheard of, as opposed to that of the English crown during the same period. Max Weber, an expert in the field of historical government and bureaucracy recognized this in his work, *Economy and Society.* He talked in detail about the changes in governmental authority over the years and recognized that with its expansion there is a converse reduction in freedoms. In 1922 he wrote:

The decisive reason for the advance of bureaucratic organization has always been its purely technical superiority over any other form of organization...however, bureaucratic administration means fundamentally domination through knowledge. (1922)

Since the paper trail in America was decidedly short in comparison to its European cousins, judges and lawyers based their decisions on very thin documentation. Eventually this developed into the "cowboy culture" of the post-Civil War 1800's western states (see *Alamo Blood and Texas Dreams--* Chapter 4). The individual was encouraged to act as both judge and jury and in some cases as executioner or arbiter of justice. It is also the result of the natural evolution of a revolutionary culture to a more stable one. Traditionally, troublemakers were effectively dealt with by "tarring and feathering." This was an unpleasant result of collective mob rule and the dispensing of quick justice through using tar and feathers to cover the offender.[10] It was used in particular against office holders and those who used bureaucratic means to push their political agenda.[11]

Since European law and established practices were older and more complex they naturally developed in a more organized fashion and were more reliant on social constructs and social justice. American law prized simplicity not as a matter of legal theory but in practical application, and when it came time to draft the Constitution, its theories were derived from those practices. While such a rural and colonial custom as tarring and feathering was not unheard of in civilized nations such as England, such aggressive justice was rare.[12]

English law was a complex bicameral process, with monarchical power being more legally complicated as it struggled to deal with the rising power of the people and the parliamentary process. The bureaucracy which had traditionally been relegated to tax collections and revenue disbursement had grown by leaps and bounds with the advent of land privatization and the challenges of industrialization. Taxation codes, business laws and moral prerogatives that were so endemic to English culture simply

---

[10] Tarring and feathering is a physical punishment used to enforce unofficial justice or revenge. It was used in feudal Europe and its colonies in the early modern period, as well as the early American frontier, mostly as a type of mob vengeance. It had the double effect of punishing the accused as well as a source of great humor for the accusers.

[11] The torture first appeared in America in Salem in 1767, when mobs attacked low-level employees of the Customs service with tar and feathers. In October 1769, a mob in Boston attacked a Customs service sailor the same way, and a few similar attacks followed through 1774 (the tarring and feathering of customs worker John Malcolm received particular attention in 1774). Such acts associated the punishment with the Patriot side of the American Revolution.

[12] One notorious exception was when, in March 1775, a British regiment inflicted the same treatment on Thomas Ditson, a Massachusetts man who attempted to buy a musket from one of the regiment's soldiers.

had no application in the American colonies and were not considered in the building of the fledgling American nation. With no king to consider, the development of an equal republic under the law was a far simpler process to both document and implement. Although Jefferson relied heavily on European philosophers and their theories to draft the first Constitution, he could not help but be a product of his own upbringing as an independent minded American landowner. While today critics suggest this was to enrich his own wallet, as well as those of the other leaders of the American Revolution, it certainly was not intentional. Jefferson could not be anything but Jefferson, and the Constitution is as much a reflection of American political theory as it is a reflection of Jefferson's own personal experiences, as well as his own religious convictions. The very notion of a legal establishment of the separation of church and state is an American concept, deeply rooted in Jeffersonian theory.[13] In his now famous Danbury Letter, Jefferson writes:

Believing with you that religion is a matter which lies solely between Man & his God, that he owes account to none other for his faith or his worship, that the legitimate powers of government reach actions only, & not opinions, I contemplate with sovereign reverence that act of the whole American

---

[13] Jefferson wrote a letter to the Danbury Baptist Association in 1802 to answer a letter from them written in October 1801. The Danbury Baptists were a religious minority in Connecticut, and they complained that in their state, the religious liberties they enjoyed were not seen as immutable rights, but as privileges granted by the legislature — as "favors granted." Jefferson's reply did not address their concerns about problems with *state* establishment of religion — only of establishment on the national level. The letter contains the phrase "wall of separation between church and state," which led to the short-hand for the Establishment Clause that we use today: "Separation of church and state."

people which declared that their legislature should "make no law respecting an establishment of religion, or prohibiting the free exercise thereof," thus building a wall of separation between Church & State. [Congress thus inhibited from acts respecting religion, and the Executive authorised only to execute their acts, I have refrained from prescribing even those occasional performances of devotion, practiced indeed by the Executive of another nation as the legal head of its church, but subject here, as religious exercises only to the voluntary regulations and discipline of each respective sect.] Adhering to this expression of the supreme will of the nation in behalf of the rights of conscience, I shall see with sincere satisfaction the progress of those sentiments which tend to restore to man all his natural rights, convinced he has no natural right in opposition to his social duties. (1802)

The legal code of early America was also developed in relationship to the early violence that preceded American independence. The concept of "right by gun" was common in colonial America with open dueling considered a legitimate legal right--although its use dwindled enormously by 1780.[14] Still, the establishment of the gun as a right was an important one to early Americans since the colonists were so reliant upon its use for not only personal defense but sustenance

---

[14] During the 17th and 18th centuries (and earlier), duels were mostly fought with swords but beginning in the late 18th century and during the 19th century, duels were more commonly fought using pistols, but fencing and pistol duels continued to co-exist throughout the 19th century.

(such as in hunting) and became essential in their struggle with England.

In the early pre-Revolution period, American colonies fought several large scale engagements in a mirror war of what was going on in Europe. The French-Indian War was a duplicate of the French and English war in Europe. Up until the English colonies began to fight as a single continent against the French armies and Indian partisans, the mere thought of American independence was only a subject of dinner table conversation. Although some political theorists of the period suggested it openly in pamphlets, they were not taken seriously as the independent minded Americans were too involved in their own internal cross squabbling of boundaries and trade issues.

At the time of the run up to the French Indian War of 1754 (also know as the Seven Years' War) neither France nor England had substantial forces stationed in North America. Some estimates put troop strengths for both sides at less than 5,000 regulars each. And yet the French were determined to establish their frontiers with the English colonies in military fashion rather than by typical negotiation and surveying. What is doubly shocking about this war was that the French population in North America at the time of the war was less than 75,000 while the English colonial population was well over a million natural born colonists. This led some historians to question the intent of the French in this land war because it had the consequence of unifying the colonies into a cohesive fighting force. But France badly needed to counter the English in some way for the war in Europe, and defending the English colonies from French raids was incredibly costly to King George, doubling his national debt. If France was planning to unify the colonies with the intent of getting the colonies to resent British troops, they could not have done a better job. By 1763, and the signing of the treaty of Paris, although France had to cede considerable territory to England, its American territories were largely uninhabited, certainly of Frenchmen and even to a lesser extent of Native American populations. According to *The Source: A Guidebook of American Genealogy* by Kory L. Meyerink and Loretto Dennis Szucs (1987) , Native American populations in the late 1790's America could not have been more than 500,000 in total among all the tribes, while the colonies of that period now topped 3.5 million easily. The striking disparity in numbers indicates that contact between colonists and Native Americans was not widespread and was limited primarily to individual encounters on the frontier. Furthermore, the huge run up of American population from 1750 to 1790 was shockingly fast and as a result, after the French and Indian and Revolutionary Wars, the American colonies considered themselves a single unit unified by war and a common cause.

The real losers in the conflict that forged America into a single nation were the limited Native American populations who were heavily displaced and now generally viewed by both sides as hostile and largely unapproachable for trade. Nations that traded with one another rarely warred upon each other and the Native American tribes were no different.

Native Americans all along the colonial borders moved further inland or in many cases were relocated by French and

British governments to islands in the Caribbean or Mexico. Without French forces to control American colonial westward expansion, they found themselves simply being out populated by colonists settling on land to which they had no legal claim in either the failing French or new American colonial governments. Interestingly enough, for a people that were supposedly exterminated by colonial expansion, Native American populations burgeoned from 1790 to 2006--from a high of five to 10 million before Spanish and French colonization, to a low of 500,000 at the time of the American Revolution, then back to 2.1 million as of 1906.[15] There is no doubt that the arrival of European colonists had a negative affect on Native American populations, but that was primarily due to Spanish and French biological contamination and illness--not America colonialism that is commonly reported.

With the French using the local Native American populations as a tool to fight their war with Europe in America, an enormous amount of hostility naturally developed between Native American populations and the now dominant English settlers. Distrust, anger and vengeance were the driving forces in hostilities and Native Americans retreated westward leaving a scorched earth policy in their wake. Less hostile tribes that had made arrangements with the French for support and supply now found themselves dependent on European and colonial support. Where it used to be a support situation that was intended to supply and support the French to fight battles, it was now replaced with a dependent lifestyle of land exchanges and reparations to

---

[15] 2000 Summary File 1 – US Census Bureau" (PDF). US Census Bureau. 2007} 2010.

Native American inhabitants that essentially made matters worse. French and British governments of the period virtually enslaved Native American populations economically, by preventing Native American tribes from living their traditional lifestyles of nomadic hunting and gathering and turning them into a poor republic in their respective empires--relying on British and French supplies of food, liquor and goods.

If there is a good analogy for the failure of government support and social programs leading to dependency, it is the story of the post-French Indian War Native American populations of North America. Reparations were initially intended to be a fair exchange of land and currency and established by the French, post-1756. But these reparations made the Native American populations temporarily protected and wealthy and as a result dependent on continued support. Entire generations of Native Americans now relied on colonial food and financial support as their nomadic and horse culture was quickly coming to an end. What some leftists today suggest as wholesale extermination of a culture was largely a matter of the basic economics behind subsidization and interbreeding, and governmental social constructs replacing a native culture. Of the approximately 4.5 million Native American people living in the continental US today, less than 2.4 million of them are full blooded.[16] Native American lands and culture were not destroyed as a matter of deliberate genocide, but rather of absorption under the mentality of "do gooders" trying to protect them, and more importantly, by the European colonial governments, not the American

---

[16] US Census Bureau, 2000 Report.

colonial expansion. Later on during the more turbulent periods of American expansion into the West, contact with Native American tribes increased, American national policy did indeed continue the European model of subsidization and reservations but by then the damage to Native American populations had already been mostly done.[17]

Evidence indicates that the more violent Native American tribes, who maintained a culture of self-sufficiency and their tribal, nomadic heritage did better in the long run, than those who capitulated and accepted help early. Today the tribes that are doing economically and societally better in America are the ones that refused colonial and European help as America expanded westward. The social constructs of the Indian Affairs bureaus and U.S. government subsidies did more to damage Native American culture and self-sufficiency than any violent actions by the American colonies or its people settling and colonizing largely vacant lands.

Compare this to the European population growth which did not have to deal with native populations in the number or type found in America. Without the wide open expansion of lands, only pre-existing failed Roman-era cities with pre-existing established roads and trade routes, European growth took on a completely different nature. As individual American governors saw power dwindle with colonization and westward expansion, European governors saw their power

---

[17] It is reasonably estimated that the total indigenous population in the Western Hemisphere declined from some 60 to 70 million—compared to over 500 million elsewhere in the world circa 1492—to as few as 5 million, then recently recovered to around its pre-Columbian levels- *Native American Demographic and Tribal Survival into the Twenty-first Century* by Russell Thornton.

conversely increase as populations grew on top of one another in massive cities and industrial complexes. The American military was engaged in dealing with uprisings of natives and the thankless job of building roads and protecting trade routes. European militaries, in comparison, focused on quelling disorder as squalor and congestion grew in its cities from overpopulation, much as the modern American armies and police forces are beginning to now adjust and deal with.

The Spanish were certainly no friend to the Native Americans either. While it is true that Native Americans traded often with their Spanish neighbors, several tribes almost faced extinction to Spanish interference in local customs and relations. The Apache tribe began dealing extensively with the Spanish for a new animal to the American Southwest--the horse. The quarter horse was not indigenous to North America. The Spanish imported them and did so in many cases exclusively to trade with Native Americans for goods[18]. As a result, tribes like the Apaches began to dominate militarily and economically their neighboring tribes and soon were the dominant Native American people of the American Southwest. Problems began to arise when the Spanish began to trade guns to the neighboring Cheyenne, Comanche and Sioux as well. This forced the Apache tribes to strike back at the Spanish colonials to both capture guns and stop the flow of weapons

---

[18] Fray Benavides, in his journals makes note of an encounter with a band of Gila Apaches and the War Chief riding a horse. This is the first time any documents refer to Native's riding horses. The Spanish allowed the natives to work with and around the animals but refused to allow them to ride them. It was forbidden to trade horses to the natives, at least by the settlers.- *Fray Alonso de Benavides's Memoriales* of 1630 and 1634

to tribes such the Lipans and Comanche (who were hostile to the Apache) with fighting that continued well into the 1780's and early 1800's. Had colonial powers like the Spanish and French not come first and developed Native American interests against European colonization and made many tribes reliant upon their trade, guns and economic supply, much bloodshed and eventual destruction of the great horse cultures of the American Southwest could have been largely avoided. Native Americans, long before the arrival of American colonists, were raiding Spanish and French settlements who they viewed as now dangerous and a threat. Americans were simply one more white man in their lands and were treated no differently, particularly since they had allied themselves with the British during portions of the American Revolution.[19]

With the pushback of the Native Americans into reservations, the consolidation of the coasts with the Transcontinental Railroad, and the final establishment of a national language of English (due to the departure of the Spanish and the French), the United States was now a nation under the singular rule of law (the Constitution) which relied heavily on the ability of its own citizens to fend for themselves on a hostile and unforgiving continent. But it was still a nation troubled by its own internal strife and the scourge of human slavery.

---

[19] In June 1777, British negotiator Henry Hamilton met with tribal leaders at Detroit and gained the support of the Chippewa and Ottawa as well as some Mingo and Wyandot. This agreement nullified the Treaty of Pittsburgh and effectively brought most Native Americans into the war on the side of the British.- West Virginia Division of Culture and History.

When the opportunity came for the Spanish and French to unload their lands to America on the cheap as settlements or purchases, they jumped at the chance. The Louisiana Purchase of 1803 was largely viewed as a land swindle perpetrated by Napoleon on America. There were few Frenchmen living in those territories and the land was rife with hostile Native Americans angry at their treatment by France and the resettlement of their people onto French reservations and islands in the Caribbean.

The lands of Texas and the Mexican Cession were also the result of European hostility with Native American tribes of the region. As the Spanish continued their policy of inter-tribal strife to control Native Americans, by the supply of guns to tribes hostile to one another, the Mexican government sought to solidify their northern border against Native American raids. Because Spain had neither the money nor the interest in protecting Mexico, the Mexican government formally asked the fledgling American government to settle in lands north of Mexico and agreed to the annexation of the Texas territory through a mutual understanding in the early 1820's. Although Mexico never formally ceded the land, it left settlers largely to their own devices to defend themselves and develop the land. The local Americans living in Texas quickly grew disillusioned with Mexican rule, believing that Mexico was deliberately leaving Texas undefended so that Native Americans would raid and damage Texas territorial lands rather than Mexico itself. They declared independence from Mexico in 1836 and requested to be a part of America by 1844, with formal treaties with Mexico which established our modern borders with that country by 1850 (see *Texas Blood and Alamo Dreams*- Chapter 4)[20]

Meanwhile American colonists in these lands had to deal with openly warring Native American tribes, and thus the border wars with tribes like the Apaches, Cheyenne and Sioux expanded. By the time American colonization had reached the lands of modern Arizona, New Mexico and Colorado, Native American tribes were wary and hostile to outside colonial peoples and dealt with the Americans in an openly hostile manner. Who could blame them after such poor treatment by the Spanish and French? Tensions escalated and the Great Plains Wars of the 1850's-1890's between the western American Indians began in earnest. This resulted in the hopelessly outgunned and outmanned Native Americans being once again forced into reservations and dependence on American economic entitlements.

Considering all of these factors, it is no wonder that American political thought developed along the lines of individualism and personal reliance and liberties rather than

---

[20] The annexation of Texas was a perfectly fair transaction. For nine years, since the victory of San Jacinto in 1836, Texas had been an independent republic, whose reconquest Mexico had not the slightest chance of effecting. In fact, at the very moment of annexation, the Mexican government, at the suggestion of England, had agreed to recognize the independence of Texas, on condition that the republic should not join itself to the United States. We were not taking Mexican territory, then, in annexing Texas. The new state had come into the Union claiming the Rio Grande as her southern and western boundary. By the terms of annexation all boundary disputes with Mexico were referred by Texas to the government of the United States. President Polk sent John Slidell of Louisiana to Mexico in the autumn of 1845 to adjust any differences over the Texan claims. But though Slidell labored for months to get a hearing, two successive presidents of revolution-torn Mexico refused to recognize him, and he was dismissed from the country in August, 1846.- *The Mexican War* by David Saville Muzzey, Ph.D. Barnard College, Columbia University, New York

social constructs and government order. This development of self-reliance is the keystone of modern American political thought and is the prime reason why the American economy today is far more vibrant than its European counterparts. Had America gone the path of European structured order, or built its society around the reparation culture as the Native Americans had, it would have been all but decimated long ago by the natural progression of European expansion. In fact, it was this theory of American independence that led France to expand her own desire for Revolution. If America had developed by a government managed and ordered societal bureaucracy it never would have moved westward. Governments would see the West as a dangerous and unmanageable frontier and best left to the Natives inhabiting it. But the individual? They saw the move West as opportunity and city streets and trails as paved with gold.

In Europe, economies were now developing along the concept of organized and planned dictates by government. Local governor's ideas of social constructs and planned economies were the order of the day, not freewheeling capitalist designs. Europe struggling under tyrants like Napoleon and whatever the king du jour offered could hardly match the westward expansion of both the American borders and its economy. In fact, Europe had largely abandoned the vast American frontiers by the time America began to move west. France was giving up the Louisiana territory from the Mississippi to the Rockies and Spain had all but withdrawn from the California and Mexican coast territories feeling that they were unconquerable and too distant and costly to manage.

It was also easy for a European city mayor or governor to determine how an economy was to develop when land purchases had to be approved by a centralized government and zoning laws were used to plan out expansion. As a result, businesses and farmers grew more slowly, having to "ask permission" before changing crops, retooling or building new factories. Americans by contrast simply did as they pleased, and with an enormous amount of cheap materials and resources at its disposal, the American economy developed at almost breakneck speed compared to its European brethren. The "de-centralized" approach to expansion compared to the European model was far more efficient and reliable when it came to industrial output.

With the high speed of development and expansion westward, a frenzied need for business and technological development began. When a business had profits on the line in the amounts that American businesses had, development of new technologies became a necessity in order to remain competitive in the wide open markets.[21]

Europe took technological development in a much different manner. Since local governors already had complete control over development in order to maintain order, it also had complete control over technological developments. In post-1700 Europe, technology was controlled by national

---

[21] Nathan Rosenberg and L. E. Birdzell, Jr., _How the West Grew Rich_. New York: Basic Books, 1986.

economic and scientific craftsman guilds and town councils, rather than by the free for all American method.[22] For years European research and development, particularly in the areas of culture, music and the arts, was considered "superior" to the haphazard, but far more profitable American methods of development. Americans were earning the reputation as slovenly rubes who ignored European scientific methods, but they were far more brilliant and timely in their discoveries.

This was the net effect of the profit motive in American culture and business, and the speed at which Americans did almost anything was cause for great disdain and disfavor in the more planned and polite European circles. Government planned "inventioneering" rarely had the success of a spontaneously developed design.

The problem with the planned technologies of Europe led to a general state of disrepair of both technologies and political development. A city mayor or governor who was a product of the system as well as a participant was far less eager to try new methods or move into new endeavors, even if the potential for increasing their influence was manifest. Thus European development fell into a genuine malaise compared to America. Additionally the Napoleonic wars were expanding and raging across the continent as cultures struggled to control the largely city based power. Battles revolved around the control of industries and destruction of

---

[22] Guilds were organizations of merchants and craftsmen. All self-employed carpenters, for example, in a town or region would comprise a guild. The guild drew up rules for the profession, elected officials, and had a treasury. Only members of the carpenters' guild could practice carpentry.

armies, rather than the traditional acquisition of land and factories. Many cities were simply blown apart by cannon fire--and along with it any chance of keeping up with American development.

The American Constitution was a product of its own success as a colonial nation and one that relied heavily on the strength of its own intestinal fortitude rather than that of a centralized government--and on its faith in God rather than its King. Colonial America was fast becoming the American nation known as the United States, bound together by simple Constitutional law, borders that reached ocean to ocean, and a unified culture of English speaking men and women building a free society based on democracy and capitalism and not on the binding restrictions of a statist and socially constructed country. She had developed a simple legal code, a common language and firmly established legal borders as early as 1850, less than 100 years into her existence--a process that took nearly a thousand years for most other European nations to match.

It was not until America began to struggle with its own Civil War that Europe could catch up. However, by the time of our own War of the States, as it was called at that time, the course of American economic development and the culture and legal codes was markedly different in their perspectives from Europe. It was only natural that Europe managed to barely keep its head above stagnation during this period, while America began to explode again post-Civil War, and the issue of a nation divided by slavery was finally resolved.

Thomas Purcell

4 ALAMO BLOOD AND TEXAS DREAMS

"Well I'm done with this here Congress and I'll see you all in Hell. As for me, I'll be in Texas" – Davy Crockett address to Congress in 1835 on his departure for Texas.

Once the French had virtually given up on the theory of Native American instability as a dividing tool in the new English colonies and sold off their interests to fund conquests in Europe under Napoleon, America turned westward to face the problem of the now faltering Spanish colonialism which was pressing an increasing the hostility of the Native Americans against European colonists.

By 1799 Spain had its own problems with the Mexican rebellion and they had lost all interest in plumbing the rich lands for the mythical Aztec gold. The locals living in the northern Mexican territories had been thoroughly infiltrated by Spanish Basques and fed by the local interests of freedom much in the same way America had just a few years earlier.[23] The large influx of Basques from their native Spain contributed greatly to the moves of Mexican independence

---

23 Basque immigration peaked after the Spanish Carlist Wars in the 1830s, and in the 1860s following the discovery of gold in the foothills of the Sierra Nevada mountain range of Northern California. The current day descendants of Basque immigrants remain most notably in this area and across the Sierras into the neighboring area of northern Nevada, then northward, into Idaho. When the present-day states of California, Arizona and New Mexico were annexed by the US after the Mexican-American War (1848).

from the original colonizing mother country of Spain. Millions of Basque descendants now live in North America (the United States and Mexico; Canada mainly in the provinces of New Brunswick and Quebec), Latin America (in all 23 countries), Southern Africa and Australia, but the largest populations still live in the Western United States. This mass migration of Basques to the plains of North America has often been referred to as the 'Basque diaspora' of the 1700's. Most of the Basques resettled parts of Mexico, thoroughly intermingling with native populations of American Indian tribes and Spanish, Aztec and Mayan peoples. Many Basques fled to the America's for the same reasons the English Puritans and other groups did; religious persecution. As a result, the Spanish Basques that intermingled with local populations were fiercely independent of their Spanish European counterparts and contributed greatly to the establishment of a lifestyle similar to their Caucasian counterparts to the north. The explosion of the Basque population also led to many in the localized Spanish army units defecting or mutineering against their Spanish European masters.

The Mexican War of Independence was far less bloody than the American Revolution, mainly because the bulk of the Spanish army had switched alliances late in the war seizing most of the lands from lower Mexico to the current California coastline. By 1822 after numerous in fights and junta wars, Mexico settled on a new emperor/dictator (Iturbide) and peace settled over the Mexican states—in no small part due to the widespread influence of Basques in Spanish American lands as well Mexico and Central America.

The problem for the Spanish colonists was that Mexico was far less settled and developed than their English (American) settlements counterparts. More rugged in territory as well as the unrelenting hostility of the natives to the Spanish caused the local population of Spanish Mexican cities to be more spread out and less industrialized.

As a result, the Mexican dictator Iturbide made a tacit agreement with the Americans to the North--settle the lands from Texas to Colorado to quiet down the Native Americans living there, and act as a buffer between the United States to the northeast and the various Mexican states to the south and the legions of hostile Native Americans in between.[24] The case of American colonial emigration into the Texas territory which eventually resulted in the Texas revolution and its eventual incorporation into the United States is a matter of some debate of historians with some believing the mass immigration into the lands was a deliberate attempt to control and colonize those lands by the American government.

However, historical records and evidence indicates otherwise, with numerous Mexican documents supporting American documentation that the more common thesis of most American emigration into the land was by direct fiat of the Mexican government.[25] In fact, the Mexican policy at the

---

[24] Hoping that more settlers would reduce the near-constant Comanche raids, Mexican Texas liberalized its immigration policies to permit immigrants from outside Mexico and Spain.

[25] Under the Mexican immigration system, large swathes of land were allotted to *empresarios* who recruited settlers from the United States, Europe, and the Mexican interior. The first grant, to Moses Austin was passed to his son Stephen F. Austin after

time of Iturbide in regards to Texican lands was astonishingly similar to that of modern American policy—namely a 'turning of heads' toward immigration across Texican borders in an effort to bolster populations and provide labor and management.

Americans poured into the gap between the two countries. They were lured by the promise of free lands and the opportunity to live more freely in open range rather than the civilized and federalized lands of the American States. As odd as it might sound, in the years after the American Revolution (1787-1824), many Americans began to view the new Federal government as a bit of a thorn and an obstacle to freedom and wide open capitalism. Although by today's standards the laws of the period were loose, people that had grown up on the American frontier as pioneers saw it differently. [26]

There was a vast difference between the pioneers' ideology about wealth from their brethren who lived in the now burgeoning eastern cities, and it gives us a good understanding about why elements of modern society are frustrated with government. Modern Americans see the same disparity between capitalism and growth from government intrusion in arguably the same way--as an obstacle not a true driver of wealth as the left wing currently contends. What most people in modern America fail to grasp is that at the

---

his death.

[26] Disillusioned by the policies and increasing power of the Federal government pioneer Davy Crockett decided to move to Texas and arrived in February, 1836. Crockett openly opposed the land policies of President Andrew Johnson and as a result was defeated by William Fitzgerald in the 1831 election.

time of the American expansion westward, even the hint of federal government intervention, except in the issues of protection and military defense, was widely discredited as an economic tool and arguably less effective than local legislation.

Statistically they are correct. American wealth over the years has undeniably come from two areas, the production of resources into material goods and the growth of housing and acquisition of new lands. A hard working man in 1820 moving to Texas, with enough grit, determination and hard work could become a land baron almost overnight.[27] There was little to stop a pioneer from establishing himself provided he could defend the land he was claiming as his own. As a result, American economic growth came primarily from the development of its abundant resources, not the manufacture of finished goods. The open ranges of the American West were, and still are, piles of gold to enterprising men and women who were willing to take the risks in gathering it. Timber, grasslands full of buffalo and cattle, gold and other mining interests, and eventually oil, helped to fuel the rest of the world's manufacturing factories and industrialization. It is safe to say that without American westward expansion and its skillful harvesting of its resources, Europe would have never reached its full potential of economic industrialization, to say nothing of American industrialization. While the leftist argues that America exploited and stole its wealth, in fact it was the other way around. Europe received the lion's share of

---

[27] On January 1, 1830, pioneer Jim Bowie left Louisiana for permanent residency in Texas. By the time of his marriage in 1831, Bowie had posted his wealth at a net worth of $223,000 ($4,580,000 today), mostly in seized and settled lands.

monetary gain from this period of American expansion which acted as a coal car to the European steam engine of industrialization and it was American dollars that bought manufactured goods from Europe at almost breakneck speed.

Among the disenchanted was a young Congressman and former pioneer, Davy Crockett of Tennessee. Only 48 at the time of his departure from Congress, Crockett had grown weary of Washington politics after a life building the American frontier in Tennessee. Even before his stint in Congress, Crockett was a legendary pioneer and fighter during the Tennessee Creek War and was the subject of many a tall tale told in taverns and inns across the south. Falling into disfavor in Tennessee for his refusal to support many public works projects and his public stance against President Johnson and his Indian Relocation Acts, Crockett went west into the Texas lands to rebuild a new life as a pioneer once again. With the promise of 4,800 acres of free land, Crockett signed aboard to help with the now growing Texas Revolution against Mexico. Although Johnson's moves were minor in comparison with the French and Spanish relocation efforts and policies, Crockett nevertheless took odds with the President and felt the need to move west and start anew.

With the fall of Iturbide and the rise of Santa Anna as the new Mexican dictator, the situation had grown dire in Texas for the Americans who had been promised lands and freedom in exchange for being a buffer against Native American raids. The Native Americans were largely peaceful to their American neighbors but the Mexican (formerly Spanish) settlements were a different matter, and now that the Native Americans were once again cohabitating peacefully with the American settlers, Mexico was clamping down on the Texians (as they called themselves) with increased taxation and governance. Considering the bulk of the settlers had come to Texas to be free of just such governance, this did not go over very well. Large land barons such as Sam Houston and Stephan Austin were now actively seeking separation from Mexico and pioneers like Crockett were paid handsomely in lands for their support.

Frontiersman Jim Bowie had come to Texas for much of the same reasons as Crockett, but he had arrived a few years earlier and established himself as a land baron. The pioneers that settled Texas were not about to give up their newfound wealth and freedom, and tensions mounted considerably from 1830-1832. By the time Crockett got to Texas in 1836 open fighting had already begun.

Various factions of Texicans decided to hold the small fort at San Antonio de Bexar (now San Antonio) in February of 1836, locally known as the Alamo. Santa Anna was moving northward with his armies, and his was a formidable force. While Houston and Austin moved northward to build an army that could defend Texian lands, Bowie, Crockett and Colonel Mack Travis decided to hold the fort at the Alamo as long as they could to buy time for the fledgling Texian army. Colonel James Fannin was sent to reinforce the Alamo in hopes of holding the fort for a few months until Houston could return with the Texian regular army.

Fannin was ambushed out on the prairie by elements of Santa Anna's main force, and the 200 or so pioneers still trapped at the Alamo decided to hold their ground. The reasons as to why they did not cut and run are unclear to this day. Some say they did not know of Fannin's failure in the Grass Fight (as it came to be known), others suggest it was just out of sheer willfulness. One thing is clear--the group of Alamo defenders knew they were certainly hopelessly outmatched and yet they still decided to stay and try to buy as much time as possible for Houston.

The battle is probably one of the most critical establishing events in American history, although at the time it certainly was not considered to have been important (except to perhaps Houston and his building Texian army). The importance of this event lies chiefly in the fact that for the first time since the American Revolution, a group of Americans decided to hold their ground and defend what they felt was rightfully – and legally- theirs despite overwhelming odds against them. The Texians numbered only 200 men in the Alamo while Santa Anna's force exceeded 5,000, and by some accounts as much as 7,500 men, with Santa Anna carrying heavy artillery and expert military training. Leftists will argue that American's stole the land but for comparison imagine if the United States Army today marched into Los Angeles and demanded that most of the Hispanic populations surrendered their businesses and homes and property to the government since their forbears had come here illegally. It would be probably met with essentially the same resistance, and the Texican claims were even more legitimate than current ones.

The pioneers and ragtag group of Americans held their ground for seven days against the massive Mexican army inflicting casualties at an almost three to one rate before finally falling to Santa Anna. Most accounts put the survivors at less than ten Americans, who were summarily executed by the livid Santa Anna angry at the enormous cost of the conquest, the unique stubbornness of the Alamo defenders, and his delay at crushing the Texian rebellion in a single swift stroke.

This is the definition of the uniquely American narrative. Americans, despite overwhelming odds and unyielding brutality, failed to give their enemy the satisfaction of an easy victory, and as a result, Houston and Austin were able to eventually outmaneuver Santa Anna and force his surrender. That surrender gave the Texas territory from Louisiana to the California coast as a settlement for the Alamo massacre and Santa Anna's defeat. Had those pioneers not acted in a rebellious and defiant manner at the Alamo, the United States borders would look much different today. Santa Anna would most certainly have caught up with Houston and Austin building their armies and decimated them in short fashion. As a result, the Texican revolution would have failed, and the United States, soon to be consumed in a Civil War , would never have had the manpower or wherewithal to resettle the lands.

This event also created another consequence--the territory of Texas, seeking protection from future Mexican incursions folded itself into the United States and eventually became a state in its own right in 1845, shortly before the Civil War. Texas joined the war on the side of the Confederacy, after deposing then Governor Sam Houston, who opposed the Confederacy.[28] Houston's argument and narrow loss of the state to the Confederacy as opposed to entry into the Union is of importance—Houston and most of the original Texicans saw slavery as anathema to good governance. Although a substantial amount of the popular vote was pro Confederacy and the state legislature had its racist elements, the traditional Texan leadership that fought the battle to free the territory from Mexico were not slave owners nor supported slavery. Most Texican leadership fledthe United States to set up a free nation outside the United States. As a result, the Confederacy which was a better representation of states' rights over federal authority, was much more in line with what Texas was trying to accomplish.

Although for some it was not an issue of slavery being profitable as it much was with Texan independent ideals, in the end, the label of Texas as a pro-slavery state stuck with them even to modern day. As a result leftists today portray Texans as backward bumpkins, racist and of limited intelligence and cowboys, despite manifest evidence to the contrary.

---

[28] Sam Houston eulogized Austin as the "Father of Texas". Later during the American Civil War many Texans considered Houston the "Traitor to the Republic" for his efforts to keep Texas from seceding from the Union and his refusal to take an oath of allegiance to the Confederate States.

The importance of the Texican Revolution and subsequent independence from Mexico and absorption into the United States cannot be underestimated, nor can the sacrifice of its people at the Alamo. It also marked the end of the age of the pioneers, with the remaining most famous pioneers of Crockett, Bowie, Travis and John Bonham lying dead in the ashes of the burnt and conquered Alamo. But the spirit of the pioneer lives on in Americans today. "Remember the Alamo" was a catchphrase used for years, not to remember or honor the fall of the fort, but to respect and revere what those men stood for. Per the Texas Military Forces Museum:

One of the most gallant stands of courage and undying self-sacrifice which have come down through the pages of history is the defense of the Alamo, which is one of the priceless heritages of Texans. It was the battle-cry of "Remember the Alamo" that later spurred on the forces of Sam Houston at San Jacinto. Anyone who has ever heard of the brave fight of Colonel Travis and his men is sure to "Remember the Alamo." (Camp Mabry, Austin Texas)

They stood for the American Way, the pride of a people to do as they wish in a free and open manner without interference or governance by either the masses or a dictatorial authority. Local Texican settlers moved westward to avoid the specter of federal oversight, intervention and power and establish a truly independent state. If Texas had not been able to establish its independence, it's likely America would have stagnated economically, and never pushed westward into the territories of Arizona, New Mexico or northwest into the Rockies except as a method to get into the ports of California.

When Americans act in this manner, in a "cowboy culture" mentality, this is not an act of instability or irreverence--it is the act of defiance against tyranny. This is the very definition of American Exceptionalism[29]; that by defining themselves in this way it gives hope to those that follow them that tyranny cannot live for long when the people simply say, "No." It is the fierce and unswerving defense of liberties even under the presence of overwhelming force, violence or economic forces that Americans have relied on for years that is represented by this ideology . It is not a hatred of government or a defiance of law that motivates this sentiment but a love of liberty and freedom. This mentality directly lived on after the battle of the Alamo as well as in the great emigration of settlers into the Midwest and eventually the modern libertarian movement, as we will soon see.

The Alamo battle was the example of the American standard of independence and it also represented the last time Americans fought for states' rights over the oversight of federal power before the advent of the Civil War which settled the matter once and for all. While Texas eventually would become part of the Union, it is for this reason that when the rest of the country settles into economic doldrums,

---

[29] American Exceptionalism refers to the theory that the United States is qualitatively different from other states. In this view, America's exceptionalism stems from its emergence from a revolution, becoming "the first new nation," and developing a uniquely American ideology, based on liberty, egalitarianism, individualism, populism and laissez-faire economics.- Lipset, Seymour Martin, *American Exceptionalism*, pp. 17-19, 165-74, 197

Texas is typically the last state to feel it, the first to recover from it and suffer the least during periods of recession.

The end result of the battle of the Alamo and America's move westward has been interpreted by leftist movement as America illegally emigrating to Mexican lands and then stealing the land from its rightful owners. Groups like La Raza assert the events in this context in their reinvention of American history. The reason for this is obvious—the actual facts present American southern expansion as critical to its economic and national security, and the battle of the Alamo the lynchpin of that expansion.

Destroy and discredit that, and you can discredit the real truth about American Exceptionalism.

4 WORKING FOR THE COMPANY STORE

The blunting effects of slavery upon the slaveholder's moral perceptions are known and conceded the world over; and a privileged class, an aristocracy, is but a band of slaveholders under another name -- Mark Twain

The American Civil War was the final building block that America needed to truly stand in the same league as its European counterparts as a world power. It was one of the few wars in human history that truly served a noble purpose-- the elimination of human slavery, and it established once and for all the nature of a centralized American government over its individual States' authority.

By 1850, America knew it was a house that was largely divided by its own inherent strengths of individual statehood, and the flaw of slavery. Even in the formation of the original constitution, the Founding Fathers addressed the inequities of slavery and its very existence was anathema to the precepts of America being a free society. America's Constitution was established to show that all men were created equal, that no man stood better than one another by reason of birth or background. Yet many states still used slaves to tend their crops and build their economics. It was clear from the outset that without some states retaining their right to slavery, no nation could be formed in post-Revolutionary America. American Exceptionalism is largely criticized today for allowing slavery to exist in its constitution in 1787, but the critics fail to recognize that without such allowances, America would have fallen into largely anarchic independent states rather than a nation and might never have thrown off slavery as an economic engine. The leftists will argue that America's power was built on slave-owner Southern economics, but the indeed the opposite is true. America's huge economic might primarily came AFTER the slave owning South was broken.

The Constitution of 1787 and the issues of slavery were hotly debated at the time of the founding of America. There was no question under the primary form of American government that slaves would be allowed to vote. The problem was that northern political leaders were concerned that slaves would be manipulated into voting in favor of more onerous and obscene slave laws in the highly populated southern states, and thus slavery would never be eliminated. The concept of a three-fifths vote was then established, not to demean the individual slave or as an act of racism, but to protect slaves from their own slave owners. With a reduced vote, slave owners were less inclined to use their slaves as a voting block to veto potential changes to slave law but were better represented against the free populations of the northern states in the House and in the general voting bloc.[30]

---

[30] The Three-Fifths compromise was a compromise between Southern and Northern states reached during the Philadelphia Convention of 1787 in which three-fifths of the population of slaves would be counted for enumeration purposes regarding both the distribution of taxes and the apportionment of the members of the United States House of Representatives. It was proposed by delegates James Wilson and Roger Sherman. Delegates opposed to slavery generally wished to count only the free inhabitants of each state. Delegates supportive of slavery, on the other hand, generally wanted to count slaves in their actual numbers. Since slaves could not vote, slaveholders would thus have the benefit of increased representation in the House and the Electoral College. The final compromise of counting "*all other persons*" as only three-fifths of their actual numbers reduced the power of the slave states relative to the original southern proposals, but

The effort was largely wasted, because until the Civil War, American federalism was largely seen as an intrusive method of changing laws, and states' individual rights were sacrosanct, as the founding fathers had originally intended. As the American populations grew and the influence of each state's economy began to affect each other, slavery and states' rights soon were falling more and more subservient to federal claims of authority. The Commerce clause of the Constitution[31] was increasingly being used to regulate and tariff trade between the states and feed the growing needs of the federal government, even insofar as the modest Indian trade was concerned.

Today many critics claim that it was slavery that was driving American economic growth until the Civil War, and America was built on the blood of slaves. A careful examination of American Gross Domestic Product (GDP), both pre and post-Civil War, suggests otherwise. In 2009 dollars, the average American's GDP in 1860 (the last year recorded before the Civil War) was approximately 4,200 adjusted dollars. Once slavery was abolished and equalization of the races started to take hold by 1901, a mere 30 years after the Civil War, American per capita GDP was nearly 9,000 adjusted dollars, and by 1918 it was over 12,000 adjusted dollars.[32]

---

increased it over the northern position.

[31] The Commerce Clause is an enumerated power listed in the United States Constitution (Article I, Section 8, Clause 3). The clause states that the United States Congress shall have power "To regulate Commerce with foreign Nations, and among the several States, and with the Indian Tribes."

[32] Source GNP: US Dept. of Commerce, National Income and Product Accounts

The reasons for this are various, but central to all of those reasons was the collapse of slavery due to the Civil War. The period of years from 1870 to 1900 was called the "Gilded Age" of American economics, but from 1780 to 1860 the slave culture of the South's technology and productivity was largely flat. While individual landowners and slave owners on the whole were wealthier than their "Gilded Age" counterparts, productivity of the overall economy was far greater in the North and could hardly compare to a slave centralized production.[33]

Slavery is, in essence, extremely cheap labor. The costs of slave ownership were primarily limited to the acquisition of the slave and room and board under conditions that would be considered well below modern-day standards of poverty. It was NOT 'free'. Because the costs of slave ownership were so low, and slaves so plentiful[34], it made land and economic development cheap. There was no driving need to improve technologies and productivity. The southern plantation owner of the period could grow and till large amounts of crops but growth came in the form of owning more land and owning more slaves—not by developing new technologies to get more yield per acre. This provided a supply that was much more than could be sold at market and the profits remained obscenely high. A plantation owner with a field of slaves to

---

[33] By 1860, on the eve of Civil War, almost 16% of the people lived in cities with 2500 or more people; and a third of the nation's income came from manufacturing. Urbanized industry was limited primarily to the Northeast during this period.- *Industrializing America: The Nineteenth Century* (1995) by Walter Licht

[34] Slave populations in 1860 were estimated at almost 4 million- "The Civil War and Reconstruction" by Randall and Donald (Their source was US Census, 1860, Population, pp. 598-599)

work the land had enough wealth to purchase or obtain just about any luxury or convenience they desired, and they had more than enough land to develop. In essence, the standard economics of capitalism and the profit motive were removed from the equation and the southern states fell into a state of stagnation and largesse. The flat economic growth and empty luxurious lifestyle of the separation of people into classes were primary reasons the South lost the war to their northern neighbors. More importantly, it led to a significant hostility of their northern neighbors and the federal government as taxation and regulation of these industries increased.[35]

In 1860, the northern states were more self-sufficient and relied more on economic development of wages and industry. They developed new and more advanced factories and farming techniques since they could not rely on cheap slave labor. However by the end of the Civil War, as slavery was abolished and condemned, world resource prices plunged which almost led to an economic collapse of foreign economies by 1875. Cotton prices overseas halved almost instantly upon Dixie's loss to the Yankees because northern Reconstructionist factions were now developing the South's cotton fields with better technology and farming techniques that were developed to compete with the South in pre-Civil War America. The collapse of cotton pricing and decimation of the previous wealthy plantation owners resulted in significant gains overall for the American economy. In 1860 the Federal government was collecting revenues of approximately 64.6 million dollars in taxation. By 1890 the

---

[35] Taxation from 1850-1860 of various tariffs increased by nearly 25%.

reinvention of a slave economy into an industrialized one was nearly completed. Those revenues were now well over 470 million dollars, despite the fact that economic technology and Federal taxation schedules of 1860 being little different than those of 1890[36]. The expansion of northern farming and manufacturing techniques into raw southern lands is largely responsible for that.

The North, due to the lack of cheap slave labor, also had to haul goods over further distances than Southern states, which could simply grow their own food supplies locally. Modern day liberal theory suggests locally grown food and supplies is more efficient and beneficial, but the historical record of American economic development shows this to be in error. Northern states developed much more extensive transportation and communication methods such as steam locomotion and telegraphy. The technologies were a boom to post-Civil War America when these largely northern technologies were applied to the wide open farmlands of the South. Cheaper cotton prices (which also had been elevated in collusion by Dixie cotton farmers) meant factories could now mass produce textiles and other goods for sale overseas rather than selling the cotton itself. The emancipation of slaves meant a plentiful supply of inexpensive labor to the north from people used to harsher working conditions who typically would work harder, longer and for lower wages than had been traditionally paid. A man lifting a bale of cotton to sell for a dollar could feed himself, but a man who gives that bale to a hauler on a steam train who sells it for 10 dollars

---

[36] Source: usgovernmentrevenue.com

feeds not only himself but everyone else along the food chain bringing that bale to market.

The economies of both the North and South now exploded in post-Civil War America, and it was mostly due to the collapse of slavery. America was not built on slave labor-- it had been held back by theories of a more localized economy and ultra-cheap labor driven by slavery. These are the very theories that are developing and being promoted today as a method to economic expansion. By keeping people tethered to land either by the ball and chain such as in the 1860 plantation south, or by modern day "green" policies and government subsidies, a nation artificially creates stagnation and economic ennui. Profits and economic growth come from the movement and exchange of goods, not by barter and exchange or locally controlled interests.

Many modern economists promote civic planning and social constructs around localization of farming and controlling the living and working conditions through regulation rather than by free market forces. The discouragement of suburbanization and agribusiness is acclaimed as a method to live a simpler lifestyle and thus be more profitable. But American Exceptionalism and experience has shown this method to be false and while it may be appealing on the surface to political standards, in the long haul it is antithetical to economic expansion and destructive to the overall quality of life in America.

The Civil War forced the North to institute a series of banking laws that allowed them access to cheap money and cash flow to buy weapons and goods from overseas. President Lincoln developed a national banking system and pushed for protective tariffs to be placed on goods made overseas, making American made goods cheaper to the average consumer.[37] Methods of mass production, industrialization, scientific management and quality control expanded greatly in post-Civil War America mainly because there was not enough cheap labor to meet the demands of the explosive population growth of 1870-1920 America, even with the introduction of nearly four million slaves into the labor pool. These methods of production had to-- there was no other way to meet the dual demands of goods and profits by the new group of industrialist tycoons gaining sway over the American economic landscape.

The dragging effect of ultra-cheap labor such as slavery is mimicked today in modern agriculture and business with the availability of large amounts of illegal immigrant labor. The flattening of middle class wages, quality of goods and costs of resources, are all artificially being flattened by the massive influx of illegal immigration, primarily from areas such as Mexico, Guatemala and other third world Central American countries. As long as massive amounts of cheap labor are available to modern agribusiness (as well as other industries), there is little to no need to push forward with technologies

---

[37] In December 1861, President Lincoln's own financial plan was presented by Treasury Secretary Salmon Chase and by Lincoln himself. Its measures included a nationally regulated private banking system, which would issue cheap credit to build industry; the issuance of government legal-tender paper currency; the sale of low-interest bonds to the general public and to the nationally chartered banks; the increase of tariffs; government construction of railroads into the middle South, and promoting industrialism over the Southern plantation system- per Abraham Lincoln's "Bank War" by Anton Chaitkin, 1986.

that would be relatively expensive to develop and use compared to immigrant labor. By removing the substantial effect of the profit motive from business, it has been counterproductive to economic growth.

Take for example a modern strawberry farm. These farms are still picked largely by hand, with an average worker taking between 30 minutes and an hour to fill a single flat of 10 punnets[38] (about a pint). Modern machinery that might pick strawberries at five to ten times the rate a man could pick them are still only on the drawing board mainly due to development costs which might cost hundreds of millions or perhaps billions of dollars. The end result of an automatic machine would be lower prices eventually at market for a punnet of strawberries and higher wage jobs for people to sell, repair and maintain the equipment. But there is no driving reason for business to use or develop these machines because labor is still cheap and available; thus the profit motive is substantially reduced.

Those that are promoting massive amounts of illegal immigration are doing so to maintain their own power and authority over their fellow man. The claim is made by liberals that immigration is the engine that builds American industry, and thus more immigration or an open border policy is the only path to increasing economic growth once again. Leftists point to our history with only a cursory understanding of how American growth was ultimately achieved, and regard the illegal immigration problem as a link to prosperity. Instead,

---

[38] A punnet is a small container or basket for strawberries or other fruit.

prosperity is not achieved by massive immigration but by the profit motive. The aspect of the large influx of labor and immigration is the **result** of the prosperity not the reverse. People from around the world, particularly the European nations of Ireland, Italy and Germany, were emigrating to the United States to flee the poverty of their own nation and to participate in America's growth and wealth. While immigrants are certainly important to growth, they are not the cause of growth but the **result** of that growth.

Prosperity from immigration was definitely an element to America's economic success during the Gilded Age in post-Civil War America, but inherent was the element of legality and integration through the theory of the "Melting Pot."

The theory of the American Melting Pot came from French writer J. Hector St. John de Crevecoeur who wrote in 1782:

*"...whence came all these people? ...Here individuals of all nations are **melted** into a new race of men, whose labors and posterity will one day cause great changes in the world.... They are a mixture of English, Scotch, Irish, French, Dutch, Germans, and Swedes... What, then, is the American, this new man? He is neither a European nor the descendant of a European; hence that strange mixture of blood, which you will find in no other country. I could point out to you a family whose grandfather was an Englishman, whose wife was Dutch, whose son married a French woman, and whose present four sons have now four wives of different nations. He is an American, who, leaving behind him all his ancient*

prejudices and manners, receives new ones from the new mode of life he has embraced, the new government he obeys, and the new rank he holds. . . . The Americans were once scattered all over Europe; here they are incorporated into one of the finest systems of population which has ever appeared." (Letters from an American Farmer)

Illegal immigration stands in direct opposition to the Melting Pot theory where immigrants were encouraged to integrate themselves with a homogenous American culture. This is not to say they would not retain their own cultural identity but rather make it part of a much greater whole.

An illegal immigrant, one that comes to America through means that would prevent normal integration, is problematic to modern American economic growth and prosperity. An illegal immigrant cannot partake in legal economic forces such as unionization, pensions or benefit from the technology of modern banking theory. They cannot borrow money in a profitable way to own a business or hold credit to provide short term capital except through illegal means. They are excluded from communications by the limits of not knowing the language, and they become isolated and insulated from American culture thus becoming hostile and resentful of neighbors moving forward.

The hostility between modern pro-Hispanic political action groups mirrors that of Civil War abolitionist political action groups, but oddly enough the anger is focused in different directions. Groups like La Raza blame Americans for perceived racism and blame America's record for Hispanic community mistreatments,[39] but fail to see that the solution of open borders and free immigration would only exacerbate the problem. Some theorists go so far as to suggest that such open hostility is actually encouraged by these groups in order to maintain the status quo and foster racial tensions to maintain their own power.[40]

Today those groups[41] also contend that the Constitution and American law are, by their very nature, a racially charged and pro-slavery set of documents arguing that the Constitution is essentially institutionalized slavery and limiting open immigration and establishing legal borders to the country enforce American Caucasian superiority.

Frederick Douglass, an abolitionist and former slave argued otherwise. Although he originally contended that the Constitution was indeed racially biased and pro-slavery, he came to understand the early American set of laws as largely just the opposite. In 1851, Douglass merged his North Star newspaper with Gerrit Smith's Liberty Party Paper to form the Frederick Douglass' Paper which was published until 1860. Douglass came to agree with Gerrit Smith, his contributing editor and business partner, as well as Lysander Spooner, a political philosopher of that period, that the United States

---

[39] "Brotherhood unites us,....A people whose time has come and who struggles against the foreigner "gabacho" (derogatory term for whites) who exploits our riches and destroys our culture- Alurista, "El Plan Espiritual de Aztlán' a manifesto advocating Chicano nationalism and self-determination for Mexican Americans

[40] The theory of *Reconquista is* the right of Mexico to reclaim land in the southwestern United States. It is officially denounced by the NCLR (La Raza) but promoted by more extremist groups.

[41] Other groups that support the concept of Reconquista include the Mexica Movement and Voz de Aztlan.

Constitution was indeed an anti-slavery document. This was actually a reversal of his opinions expressed with William Garrison that it was pro-slavery (he had once burned copies of the Constitution in protest), and Douglass elaborated extensively on this opinion in Spooner's book *The Unconstitutionality of Slavery* in 1846. Douglass went further than most abolitionists of the time by even saying that the Constitution could and should be used as an instrument in the fight against slavery.

These facts are often ignored by modern illegal immigration proponents and advocacy groups who use Douglass' earlier work to promote the issue of the Constitution as a racially motivated document that promotes slavery. Leftist groups direct their arguments to American law, which established its borders through illegal purchases as a country, arguing that America established itself by rule of slavery and the genocide of the Native American peoples, which is factually inaccurate (see Chapter 3).

The constant promotion of an influx of immigrants who could not by default become normalized members of American society is making matters worse rather than better. Slavery and a plentiful supply of cheap labor below normal economic supply and demand (such as legal immigration and non-slavery sharecropping) actually contributes to economic stagnation and a flattening of overall wages.

The more illegal immigration becomes the norm in America, the more America will resemble a third world country with all of its resulting problems. Only when an immigrant comes to America and adopts the American work ethic, American labor standards and lives under the protection and equality of its law, does the immigrant stand to become part of America.

An article in the New York Times[42] discussed the realities of living in the United States as it relates to income, in regards to a new book *The Haves and the Have-Nots*, by the World Bank economist Branko Milanovic about referenced United States income rates as it relates to the rest of the world and the separation of wealth in the United States. It came to the conclusion that wealth is related to where you are born not what you do with your life; and that being born in some countries is a penalty to wealth accumulation. While that is largely true, it misses a key point, that while the separation of wealth exists in the United States between the average citizen and the very wealthy, it is by far a flatter curve than in virtually every other country—and most importantly, that even the poorest in America lives in far better living conditions that even many wealthy people do in foreign nations.

It is an inescapable conclusion that while America's poorest people are in many cases wealthier than the wealthiest Indian or most of China, its conclusion that wealth is based on the nation of birth misses an important truth--that American style capitalism is responsible for the highest average standard of living in the world, not the Communist countries of China, nor the planned economy of Brazil, both of

---

[42] *The Haves and the Have-Nots* By Catherine Rampell, January 31, 2011.

which are touted as models for the future of the American economy by the current administration.[43] As America moved away from its slavery roots in the South, it began to mold a new, relatively flat, wage curve where even the poorest of the poor live in better conditions and have a higher wage than even the wealthiest strata of the restricted economies of China and Europe.

The American middle class are only middle class in America. Anywhere else, they would be consider the wealthy elite.

In America even the indigents generally have access to high quality medical care (through Medicare or Medicaid),[44] clean running water, decent shelter, food and basic human necessities. There are even photos of homeless people here in America that have cell phones (yes there is a government program that provides free cell phones to the indigent[45]). The left often claims that there is no middle class any more, and that the poor get poorer, but here in America, the disparity of wealth is relatively flat compared to other nations. Another oft quoted line is that the amount of wealth in America is now falling into fewer hands than ever before. While statistically

---

[43] "Over the last decade, the progress made by the Brazilian people has inspired the world. More than half of this nation is now considered middle class. Millions have been lifted from poverty. For the first time, hope is returning to places where fear had long prevailed" --Barack Obama address to Brazil, March 9th 2011.

[44] Over 100 million Americans are now using either Medicare or Medicaid- per MyMedicare.gov.

[45] The $4 billion a year Universal Service Fund which provides the poor, schools and library's with free cell phones is paid for by telecommunications companies. The cost is then recouped form the average American bill payer, who has a "universal service" charge added to their cell contract every month.

some element of that is true, the reason for that is as America shifts its economy into a more worldwide stance, it is going to resemble those other income curves, not because the basic tenets of capitalism are somehow flawed, or that traditional American economic theory is inherently wrong.[46] The wealth of America's millionaires does not come from wages, but from entrepreneurship , investment and capitalist expansion. Even the American tax code recognizes this and thus (rightly so) taxes capital gains at a lower tax rate than wages and ordinary income.

America currently is the largest manufacturer of goods worldwide while China limps along at a second place that is barely half of America's manufacturing power. Keep in mind too that America is in her worst economic slump since the Great Depression of 1929, and is producing GDP at levels that are marginally above that of 1998. Even when we are flat broke, we are still an economic engine that can steamroll any other economy in the world, and the United States was built on capitalism, not on a socially planned and regulated economy like Brazil or China. Furthermore, had America continued along as a split nation of slavery, it never would have accomplished as much as it has.

The issue here is not that wealth is based on where you were born but under what economic system your country operates. Most of the European Union and South American countries operate on planned economies. Brazil's income

---

[46] Most of that income of the top 1% does not come from "working": in 2008, only 19% of the income reported by the 13,480 individuals or families making over $10 million came from wages and salaries. – Study Norton & Ariely, 2010.

distribution looks like Germany, France and England. They are similar in the respect that the people work under economically controlled conditions that are almost identical to the plantation rules of America in 1840. This is the sort of life that Americans will have if the current government gets its way in the marketplace with big corporations dominating an overly regulated and managed marketplace. Planned economics lead to planned failure, just as it did in the plantation South or the Five-Year Soviet Union.

Economic inequality and governmental planning explains why many countries with sealed borders are injurious to international relations and profits. Countries that both have a McDonalds in them are much less likely to go to war, a strong indication that open trade encourages peace.[47] It is capitalistic endeavors like free trade, open wage rules and a minimally regulated economy that built America, not the social structuring of the 1960's nor the political forces driving it. The Confederacy used planned economics here in America as well, and it was a consummate failure.

After all, there is a reason why America builds fences to keep people out and other countries build fences to keep people in. The more we allow planned economic theories into our nation, the more we will begin to resemble the third world economies they originate from—or the slave nation of the 1860's American South.

---

[47] In The Lexus and the Olive Tree, Thomas L. Friedman coins the "Golden Arches Theory of Conflict Prevention".

America's wealth, standard of living, and long term growth has come from investment, industry and the inherent superiority of capitalism , not slavery, illegal immigration or the flawed theory that the wealthy in society did so on the backs of others.

6 THE BULLY PULPIT

A thorough knowledge of the Bible is worth more than a college education.- Theodore Roosevelt

As America grew by leaps and bounds from the Civil War Reconstruction and with the industrial and farming modernization of the South begun, the rest of the world was beginning to feel the impact of populations that had no room to expand and the corruption of powerful governments.

Europe was on the brink of war by the turn of the century as their corrupt leaders finally ran out of ideas to steal more money from their citizens and turned their greed and lust for power onto each other. Napoleon was gone, but in the power vacuum France had left behind rose the might of the Germans under the direction of the Hohenzollerns. In Russia, unrest under the Tsars was increasing and the incredible poverty of the Russian people were driving them toward reform as well.

The economic eggs that their political chickens had laid in the 1850's were now beginning to hatch across the globe.

England's colonial imperialism was now an Empire too large to manage, and the Empire that never saw the setting sun was now in perpetual twilight. The English crown's weakness was further expanded with the internal turmoil of the thrones familial woes, and Victorian England was the beginning of the end of English hegemony in the world adding more to the ever increasing vacuum left by France and Spain's dwindling power. While England under Victoria and eventually Edward was still powerful and secure, the roots of its eventual demise had now grown deep and were entrenched in English society and government.

The world was beginning to slip into chaos.

Yet America, protected by her two great oceans and huge tracts of undeveloped lands, was largely untouched by the growing chaos. Her own problems and the Civil War left her vision mostly clouded to the problems of the world, and once she emerged from the barbarity of slavery, and economic stability was restored, the United States soon found itself interested in the complexities of world politics. The creation of the US Presidency as the "bully pulpit" by which America could influence the world was still just a thought in the mind of more forward thinking individuals.

Central to this theory was the Progressive[48] Movement of Theodore Roosevelt, who saw America as the model for the world both economically and philosophically. His "big stick" polices were about to be demonstrated in a highly visible and contentious method--he was going to complete the Panama Canal--a project that for years the Europeans had wanted and had failed to accomplish. To Roosevelt, who so desperately wanted to be a 'player' in world politics and have America

---

[48] The Progressive Era in the United States was a period of social activism and reform that flourished from the 1890s to the 1920s. It is not the same movement as modern day leftist Progressive thought, although its roots are the same.

dictate the world's events, the Panama Canal represented not so much a failure for other nations as it was an opportunity for America.

If there was one emblem of that period that stands out as a model of modern American ingenuity and work ethic, it was the Panama Canal. President Roosevelt used the canal as his "big stick" in foreign policy to emphasize the power and influence of the American economic engine and to promote his theories of big government doing big things.[49] Roosevelt, the first modern progressive leader, believed that government was the be all and end all to man's problems, and certainly the only entity that could conceivably build such an enormous project as the Panama Canal. The interesting thing about Roosevelt's concept of government is that it was the early formative years of modern Progressivism which had all the idealistic jingo of a child's version of the world, and had not yet been exposed to the end results of big government—the 1940's and Nazism. Had Roosevelt seen the end results of nationalism and socialistic big government, he might not have been so eager to consider a Federal government as the solution to man's problems. Putting that aside though, Panama was where Roosevelt had decided to emblematically make a stand for American foreign policy.

For years France had been attempting to build a canal through the Isthmus of Panama with little success, even though plans to build a canal had been circulating as early as

---

[49] Roosevelt strongly supported scientific methods as applied to economics, government, industry, finance, medicine, schooling, theology, education, and even the family.

the 1700's, perhaps even as early as 1534.[50] Although train routes had been established by the 1850's across the 50 mile span, the ultimate solution to east-west cargo transport lay in a navigable waterway. The French employed renowned canal builder Ferdinand de Lesseps the famed architect and engineer that built the Suez Canal for Napoleon III. It was felt that only de Lesseps, with his experience in the Suez, could construct such a waterway.

The problem was that de Lesseps attempted to build what was essentially a duplicate of the Suez Canal in a considerably different environment. The basic engineering of the Suez was nothing but a large ditch; a canal without any locks or dams. This was adequate for cutting a swath through flat desert terrain, but through the mountainous jungles of Panama it was disastrous. Between the poor engineering and the inherent problems of malaria and dysentery that plagued the jungles of Panama, the French project was doomed and ultimately de Lesseps was convicted of bribing the government officials who funded the project, and he was scandalized with a prison sentence.

Roosevelt purchased the Canal Zone from the French for a paltry sum of 40 million dollars and the great government adventure of "Roosevelt's Canal" had begun.

American engineers quickly discovered why the French had failed and had sold out so cheaply. The French idea of a standard level canal was completely unworkable, and soon

---

[50] "A History of the Panama Canal: French and American Construction Efforts"-- Panama Canal Authority.

even the Americans were in over their heads. By 1905, chief engineer John Frank Stevens had to present Congress with a completely new plan involving an expensive and complicated "locks" system and an ingenious railroad method of excavation and removal of the millions of tons of tailings from the excavation site. To say that the Panama Canal was an engineering marvel would be an understatement, but even more of a marvel was Stevens' method of modern construction techniques which allowed him to build the canal despite massive problems and enormous technical difficulties of a lock design in a mountainous jungle.

The reason this is important is because it marked an important change in American politics—the power of lobbying and big projects with government backing. Previously, Congress had avoided large expenditures on public works, preferring to take a back seat role to massive scale public works and allowing individual states to run the show. But Roosevelt and other argued that such a stance would preclude America from joining other world powers in political domination, and now the Civil War had firmly established the legal jurisprudence of a large scale and Federal American government.

The interesting point about the canal construction, however, is that despite the marvelous engineering feats of Stevens, the canal was still faltering in both timeliness and cost. Stevens could only take so much of the deplorable and difficult working conditions, and Roosevelt brought in engineer George Washington Goethals as his replacement when Stevens bowed out. Goethals, while competent, was no

Stevens and once again the project began to stall from complaints about the loss of life to the enormous ballooning cost. While the engineering excellence and technical expertise of the engineers cannot be overstated, it took an American President with the willpower of a bulldog to finalize its success.

This was the first time an American President had done this and on so large a scale. It was Roosevelt that used the Canal to his worldwide political advantage, not Congress, and while the Presidency was legally the head of state in the world theatre (Congress is head of government), Roosevelt had leapfrogged to the head of the class with his Panama canal. The big question for Roosevelt, was the decidedly open question if the Canal would be completed in his lifetime—if ever.

It was in November of 1906 with support for the canal floundering in Congress that Roosevelt took it upon himself to personally see that the canal was once again an American priority. Congress had begun to spin the wheels of failure in the media of the time and was considering cancelling funding and plans for continuing the construction of the canal. Most of Congress saw the Canal as a worldwide embarrassment, not a success and the other European powers, in particular, France; were laughing at the US floundering in Panama. The 'see I told you so' crowd were having a field day. Despite good progress being made at that time, the cost was beginning to increase well beyond what was originally planned.

Roosevelt made the trip to the Canal Zone and visited the men working on the canal seizing the moment and understanding its historical importance beyond what Congress could envision. Fantastically, it was the first time a US president had left the United States, and Roosevelt made the most of it. Spending three weeks in the zone he involved himself with every aspect of the canal construction, from the senior staff to the five thousand workers slaving in abominable conditions. When Roosevelt returned to the United States exhausted and suffering from malaria himself, the general view of the American people in favor of the canal had dramatically turned around in its favor. The next month Roosevelt was honored by the Nobel commission with a Peace Prize, arguably for his involvement in the in ending Russo-Japanese War in 1905, and he was the first American to win the Nobel Prize in any of the six categories. Roosevelt received the award while in Europe in 1910, but realistically it was for his public and personal involvement in the building of the Canal.

The Panama Canal represents more than the sheer enormity of the engineering accomplishment. It also represented the first time an American President was now considered a world leader, and he had been honored with a Nobel Prize.[51] This developed the role of the American Presidency as more than just an administrator of the American bureaucracy, but as a defined symbol of American superiority. Despite his considered moves toward making

---

[51] Roosevelt negotiated an end to the Russo-Japanese War for which he won the Nobel Peace Prize. Roosevelt was the first American to win the Nobel Prize in any field.

America more like their European counterparts, his real contribution to American theory was the development of the American presidency in the role of a world leader rather than as an administrator of a nation of farmers.

Up until the French failure in Panama, it was France and England that were viewed as the leaders of the civilized world. More importantly, the French and English monarchs were considered the sole legitimate leaders of the world, and Roosevelt's ascension and elevation in world esteem meant Roosevelt was the first "free" man to achieve such a position of prominence. He was an elected leader, not one of birth, nobility or meritocracy, but one who represented the will of the American people. If not for Roosevelt, the symbolism of the American "bully pulpit" would be largely ignored today.

Such an achievement was not easily earned. Roosevelt suffered the rest of his life with bouts of sickness and malaria which led to his early death at the age of 60 from a blood clot which was most certainly from the complications of a lifetime bout with sickness from the Panama trip. In fact, although he contracted malaria from his 1913 safari expedition, the combination of his travels abroad and continued bouts with malaria almost certainly shortened his considerably productive life. Ironically, almost 70 years later, it was another Progressive, President Jimmy Carter that surrendered the Canal back to the Panamanians, who neither built nor encouraged its development.[52]

---

[52] . Negotiations toward a new settlement began in 1974, and resulted in the Torrijos-Carter Treaties. Signed by President of the United States Jimmy Carter and Omar Torrijos of Panama on September 7, 1977, this mobilized the process of granting the

The power of the Presidency as a world leader was also viewed with derision by his successor Woodrow Wilson (after Taft), who viewed Roosevelt as an opportunistic militarist. Wilson saw the world as his schoolteacher background had taught him too, as mostly a place to be ignored. Wilson was largely a pacifist and only got elected because Taft and Roosevelt had split the Republican vote against Wilson in the 1912 election. President Wilson's first term as President emphasized administration over world politics and leadership; founding the Federal Reserve, the IRS (Income Tax Act), farm loan subsidies and other progressive policies--progressive, not defined as Roosevelt had, but as modern political theorists understand it.[53] Although Roosevelt and Wilson were both of the same party and both big government Progressives, Roosevelt abhorred Wilson's interpretation of big government politics , which is now the root of modern Progressive thought Presidents like Carter and Obama. In fact, Roosevelt's distaste for an overreaching government and Wilson's Progressivism 'hijacking' his own ideas of Progressive politics is what led to Roosevelt attempting another run at the Presidency. Ironically, it was this very attempt that resulted in Wilson taking the White House.

Wilson's pacifist tendencies, while lauded at the time as "keeping America out of war in Europe," largely contributed

---

Panamanians free control of the canal so long as Panama signed a treaty guaranteeing the permanent neutrality of the canal. The treaty led to full Panamanian control effective at noon on December 31, 1999, and the Panama Canal Authority (ACP) assumed command of the waterway.

[53] The Progressive Party founded in 1924 and the Progressive Party founded in 1948 were less successful than the 1912 version. Today, most progressive politicians in the United States associate with the Democratic Party or the Green Party of the United States.

to the violence and enormity of World War I. Wilson failed to use Roosevelt's carefully cultivated "bully pulpit" in a manner that would have kept world peace. As the world now saw America, a power vacuum formed in Roosevelt's absence and the pacifist president found himself hip deep in the first World War, and his pacifist notions of German reparations in the armistice signed in 1918 led directly to the Second World War.

However, Roosevelt's prototype of an activist President became the mold in which most successful future Presidents began to see themselves. The success of the construction of Panama Canal is directly related to his personal willpower and ability to motivate and rally Americans around a central cause. In later years, his type of presidency is often viewed as "cowboy politics" by his detractors, initially Wilson but later on by liberal Presidents such as Jimmy Carter and currently Barack Obama.

What is interesting most about the latter liberal presidents and their opposite view of the role of the presidency is that all three had largely academic backgrounds. Wilson was a college professor at Princeton and the New York Law School, and he wrote many an opinion on Constitutional law. Wilson viewed the Constitution as unwieldy, outdated and corruptible in its inherent design. He saw the US Constitution as an obstacle to government in meeting the country's needs by enumerating rights that the government may not infringe. Wilson preferred a parliamentary system for the United States. Writing in the early 1880s:

I ask you to put this question to yourselves, should we not draw the Executive and Legislature closer together? Should we not, on the one hand, give the individual leaders of opinion in Congress a better chance to have an intimate party in determining who should be president, and the president, on the other hand, a better chance to approve himself a statesman, and his advisers capable men of affairs, in the guidance of Congress.

Wilson saw the checks and balances of the Constitution and American government as obstacles; not legitimate legal concepts or the natural evolution of a strong presidency as Roosevelt did. His book, *Congressional Government* (1885), was a treatise on how best to run America without a Congress or its bicameral system. He wrote again:

How is the schoolmaster, the nation, to know which boy needs the whipping? ... Power and strict accountability for its use are the essential constituents of good government... It is, therefore, manifestly a radical defect in our federal system that it parcels out power and confuses responsibility as it does. The main purpose of the Convention of 1787 seems to have been to accomplish this grievous mistake. The "literary theory" of checks and balances is simply a consistent account of what our Constitution makers tried to do; and those checks and balances have proved mischievous just to the extent which they have succeeded in establishing themselves. (1885)

Clearly there could not be two more different political philosophies about the role of the Presidency and American government than Roosevelt and Wilson, despite them both being Progressives believing in a strong centralized government. While Roosevelt embraced the concept of American Exceptionalism and Yankee know-how, Wilson wanted America in more of a backseat role in the world with a return to a simpler--and frankly more monarchical--government. Although some historians and authors blame Roosevelt for the rise of modern Progressivism, a more careful reading puts it in context—Roosevelt's Progressive ideas were in an age which had not seen the horrors of Nazism or Communism, which is the Progressive movement's stepchild. Instead the blame should fall on Wilson, who Roosevelt ultimately tried to stop from gaining the White House.

Years later, President Jimmy Carter once again took on the mantle of Wilsonian government deconstruction with essentially the same results of world discord and American malaise. He too had an academic's view of America's role in world affairs. After his early life in the Navy and work in nuclear engineering, he served government in various education and library committees eventually running for Congress in 1960. After serving two terms he developed his family peanut farm business and prepared for the role of Governor of Georgia serving from 1971 to 1975, which led to his presidency in 1976.

It is ironic that it was Jimmy Carter that eventually returned control of the Panama Canal back to the Panamanian people. In post-World War II Panama, there was growing discontent with the existence of the Canal in American hands, and protests were growing annually. Many

Panamanians felt that the Canal Zone rightfully belonged to Panama; student protests were met by the fencing in of the zone and an increased military presence. The unrest culminated in riots in which approximately 20 Panamanians and several US soldiers were killed on Martyr's Day (as it is called in Panama) on January 9, 1964.[54] Carter's world view coincided with the Panamanian view that American interests should not override the interests of the Panamanian people, despite the enormous cost of the building of the Panama Canal on the backs of the US taxpayers and American lives lost. As a result Carter arranged for Panama to once again control the lands inside the zone, and the Canal itself.[55] Carter's actions were counter to Roosevelt's role of American supremacy, and was met with great discontent in the American electorate, as well as Congress. A few days before final agreement on the treaties was reached, Carter had sent a telegram to all members of Congress informing them of the status of the negotiations and asking them to withhold judgment on the treaty until they had an opportunity to carefully study it. Senator Strom Thurmond responded to Mr. Carter's appeal by stating in a speech later that day, "The canal is ours, we bought and we paid for it and we should keep it."

The loss of the Canal was a public relations disaster for the White House, and was one of many factors leading to Carter's defeat to Ronald Reagan in 1980. Yet Carter

---

[54] *The Martyrs of 1964*, by Eric Jackson

[55] The Torrijos-Carter Treaty are two treaties signed by the United States and Panama in Washington, D.C., on September 7, 1977, which abrogated the Hay-Bunau Varilla Treaty of 1903.

stubbornly stuck to his liberal theories that America had perpetrated a fraud on the Panamanian people in the Canal construction, which was also the position of the Panamanian rebels hostile to America at the time, despite substantial evidence indicating Roosevelt had purchased the land legally from the French. Worse, when the handover was complete in 1999, the government of Panama held an international bid to negotiate a 25-year contract for operation of the container shipping ports located at the Canal's Atlantic and Pacific outlets. The contract was not affiliated with the ACP (Panama Canal Authority) or Panama Canal operations and was won by the firm of Hutchison Whampoa, a Hong Kong-based shipping concern whose owner is Li Ka Shing, the leading Chinese businessman in the world. Such a loss was another blow to American supremacy in the business world.

Carter's presidency mirrored that of Wilson in many ways including a dogged persistence to pursuing peace among enemies no matter the cost. As a result he is often viewed as a weak and ineffectual president. Like Wilson, an excellent administrator with a particular eye for detail, he failed to capture the public imagination of the role of the Presidency as a world leadership position. He also wanted more government control of the economy, and like Wilson's Federal Reserve, was instrumental in creating more economy-by-government. He crafted the bailout of Chrysler in 1979, and promoted and passed expansive Environmental Protection Agency (EPA) rules that widely involved government in the private sector. Most of these policies fundamentally changed the role of government in the private sector and resulted in large unemployment numbers and massive inflation with the devaluation of the dollar.

President Barrack Obama is also of the minimalist foreign policy presidency camp. Obama, a law professor by trade and community activist by reputation, also views the role of the presidency less as the world leader, and more as a team player. While history has yet to judge the role of Obama's presidency, early indications are that his decidedly minimalist view is leading to the same foreign entanglements that both Carter and Wilson suffered from. He too has re-examined the role of government in the private sector and wants a more European style economic/government partnership. Innovation, creation and technological revolution does not come from a committee or via government fiat as modern Progressivism promotes, but rather by the open exchange of ideas in a free market and private industry. Regulation and governance therefore is antithetical to these positive changes to society. This limitation of positive change causes trade to restrict and economies to falter leading to political and military instability.

Nature abhors a vacuum and the result of America's withdrawal from overseas activism is often worldwide instability. The "bully pulpit" built by Roosevelt on the banks of the Panama Canal was as much a curse as it was a blessing. When presidents fail to seize upon its mantle, as did Wilson and Carter, it leaves a terrible hole in the stability of foreign governments. Roosevelt, for better or worse, regardless of one's view of his politics, established once and for all that the American Presidency is the premier arbiter of world peace and American Exceptionalism. It was only America that could build the Canal; it would be only America that could end the wars in Europe. Had Roosevelt failed in Panama, it would have been France or England that would have continued their worldwide political hegemony. America would have been viewed as more bravado than substance and merely an element of braggadocio in a world of sensibility. The English and French crowns would have stood for stability and reason and America a nation of loudmouths and boors. This is why the surrender of the Panama canal, and the resulting expansion of Chinese interests in the Zone are highly indicative of the shifting of political as well as economic power.

But it was Theodore Roosevelt that proved to the world that America could accomplish what the rest of the world could not--and did it by the dint of sheer willpower and American ingenuity, rather than the Wilson, Carter and Obama concepts of rule by consensus and committee. Ultimately the concept of the bully pulpit and Teddy's development of big government led to the Progressivism we now know today as liberalism and leftism. But at the time, without such a driving leadership it is unlikely America would have stepped into the limelight as a world leader. It was no coincidence that the Canal was built not through administration or government planning or strategic engineering but ultimately through an American President who stood on its banks and said "Yes, we can."

The American Way: Why Superman Got It Wrong

7 THREE CHEERS FOR THE LITTLE GUY

The great poems, Shakespeare's included, are poisonous to the idea of the pride and dignity of the common man, which are the life-blood of democracy- Walt Whitman

American Exceptionalism is not limited to its leaders. After all, its leaders must come from somewhere, and that means they are born daily from among the ranks of the working, the unemployed, the lawmen and the criminals. Our greatest leaders typically have come from the children of the American frontier however, at least from an historical perspective. The American pioneering life and its dedication to hard work, self-reliance and self-determination made a fine breeding ground for men and women of character. The pioneering period from approximately 1850-1920, when Americans moved westward across the continent, proved to be the largest migration of human beings since the movement of the former peoples of the Roman empire at the time of Christ.

Without consequence you cannot breed greatness, and the settlers of the period from 1850 to 1920 could not have had known any greater hardships than their simple attempts at providing sustenance and succor for their families. Whereas today the United States provides cradle to grave protections and support, no such protections existed pre-1920. Men and women lived and died on the prairie and in many cases never saw paved roads their entire lives. Electricity, refrigeration, telephones and many other creature comforts that we take for granted today were still a generation or more away, and travel relied mostly on horse or on foot.

A key element to prairie life was the absolutely dogged determination to provide for one's own self and family. Part of the charm and attraction for many pioneers was the desire to live away from Federal government rule and oversight. America had been founded on a minimalist government and as cities and society became more complex, many fled westward into the wild open prairies to avoid its encroachment. The prevailing theory was that reliance on government was simply another form of charity; thus with freedom also would come considerable wealth and prosperity. The people of the Midwestern frontier also believed that charity was to be frowned upon as emasculating, and government charity was the worst kind left only for those that cannot fend for themselves.

Many Americans of the period actually viewed such government protections and support as a negative thing, and societal taboos existed around the acceptance of charity. Davy Crockett himself gave a speech on the dangers of government taxation and entitlements shortly before his exodus to Texas. The speech known as the "*Not Yours to Give*" speech may or may not have been directly said to Congress at the time of his departure for Texas, but it has been widely attributed to him. It revolves around a bill written by Congress to help out the widows of Navy men who were destitute. There is no written record of a debate in Congress during that period, although the record indicates that Crockett did indeed vote against a bill in 1828 for funds for the widow of the deceased General Brown. The speech would have been unlikely given regarding this bill (there are numerous inconsistencies) but the fact remains, in this case, Crockett did indeed vote against the widow's welfare and at some point may have given a speech similar or identical to this one although historians contend, with substantial evidence, that it was not in Congress during this period.[56]

Nevertheless, it is a powerful speech rumored to have turned the tide against Andrew Jackson. As a result Crockett was not re-elected. He eventually moved to Texas to start fresh and died at the Alamo protecting freedom and self-determination--the only US Congressman to have died in military action outside the United States.[57] Whether it is a tall tale or merely an exaggeration, the important point is that Crockett voted against subsidizing poverty, and for this, as well as his support for the Seminoles against the Jacksonian Indian Relocation act, public sentiment turned against him. In the speech, Crockett told a story of an old man who was explaining his principles while riding on the road one day through his district in Tennessee :

---

[56] There is a speech attributed to Davy Crockett, *Not Yours To Give* that can be found all over the internet and popular books of American folklore. It appears to have first surfaced and circulated (as legit) in print in the early 1960s among right wing tax protest groups. It even found its way into the Wikipedia entry on Davy Crockett and from there links to Texas Congressman Ron Paul's government website as a source, saying that it was originally published in "*The Life of Colonel David Crockett*," by Edward Sylvester Ellis. However, there is an historical record that supports a similar story--the House considered a bill of relief for the family of deceased general Brown in April of 1828 and Davy Crockett is on record opposing that bill and offering personal support to the family. You can read the (very brief) summary of that in the Register of Debates:
http://memory.loc.gov/cgi-
bin/ampage?collId=llrd&fileName=006/llrd006.db&recNum=308

[57] Texas was not then a state at the time of the Battle of the Alamo.

'It is not the amount, Colonel [Crockett] that I complain of; it is the principle. In the first place, the government ought to have in the Treasury no more than enough for its legitimate purposes. But that has nothing to do with the question. The power of collecting and disbursing money at pleasure is the most dangerous power that can be entrusted to man, particularly under our system of collecting revenue by tariff, which reaches every man in the country, no matter how poor he may be, and the poorer he is the more he pays in proportion to his means. What is worse, it presses upon him without his knowledge where the weight centers, for there is not a man in the United States who can ever guess how much he pays to the government. So you see that while you are contributing to relieve one, you are drawing it from thousands who are even worse off than he. If you had the right to give anything, the amount was simply a matter of discretion with you, and you had as much right to give $20,000,000 as $20,000. If you have the right to give to one, you have the right to give to all; and, as the Constitution neither defines charity nor stipulates the amount, you are at liberty to give to anything and everything which you may believe, or profess to believe, is a charity, and to any amount you may think proper. You will very easily perceive what a wide door this would open for fraud and corruption and favoritism, on the one hand, and for robbing the people on the other.'

This was a popular sentiment among the people of this period and most certainly popular among the pioneers and settlers leaving for the West. Taxpayer funded aid was considered charity and a thing to be avoided. More importantly, it was an issue hotly debated in Congress as to the authority of the Federal government to use taxpayer money for charitable purposes. It was consider, as this speech indicates, a form of robbing Paul to pay Peter with the consent and protection of government.

Since quite often the matter of life or death hinged upon the strength of one's own two hands, it became a matter of pride to make those hands as able as possible. On the prairie, under threat of Indian attack, and on top of the ordinary difficulties of harsh weather and lack of civilization, men often found it necessary to be harsh to one another in order to survive themselves. In a wagon train, if one or two men could not keep up with the work and difficulties of prairie life, it could quite possibly get the entire caravan killed as others tried to make up for the slack. It was viewed as a weakness to help a fellow wagon trainer.

Those who risked the lives of others by helping the weak earned the name of "tenderfoot."[58] Tenderfeet were to be avoided at all costs and many a tall tale revolved around tenderfeet getting entire groups of people killed.

---

[58] The California gold rush enriched the American vocabulary with "forty-niner" and with mining terms like "pay dirt," placer, sluice, and tailings. It also brought in the kind of person known as a "tenderfoot." This was a beginner or newcomer, someone unaccustomed to mining and the West. Outfitted for mining, the newcomer was likely to be costumed in his first pair of cowboy boots, which would soon make the feet tender. Another word for the phenomenon was "rawheel." as we learn from a young miner, Tommy Plunkett, who was recorded in a friend's diary in 1849 as saying, "We saw a man in Sacramento when we were on our way here, who was a tenderfoot, or rawheel, or whatever you call 'em, who struck a pocket of gold." See: http://www.answers.com/topic/tenderfoot#ixzz1UCshnnms

Although the origins of the word are unclear, tenderfoot meant that the person so named has a weakness of heart or exhibits tenderness as a personality trait. Tenderfoot behavior such as slowing a wagon train for weaker members, or trying to take an easier route to a destination in order make things easier on women or children could very well get the entire group killed. The label tenderfoot was stuck on anyone that didn't know what they were doing or was inexperienced in prairie life.

One example of a 'tenderfoot' story, that unfortunately was no tall tale, was that of the Donner Party of 1847. The Donner wagon train attempted to cross the Sierra Nevada range in the dead of winter against the advice of locals who knew the mountains well and the icy death it contained in winter months. The stories of tragedy along the route abounded, but the most significant event came in October of 1848 when the party leader George Donner led his group into the heart of the Sierra Nevada mountains along the Truckee River. While historical accounts vary as to the reasons why, there is indication he was inexperienced to believe it was a shorter route, and the snows did not begin until late November. As such, he waited too late to make the ascent and there was no doubt as to the result. The Donner party was almost entirely wiped out by hunger, cold and starvation at the head of the Truckee; snowed in until spring despite several attempts to rescue them.[59]

---

[59] Rescuers from Sacramento, California, attempted to reach the emigrants, but the first relief party did not arrive until the middle of February 1847, almost four months after the wagon train became trapped. Forty-eight of the 87 members of the party survived to reach Sacramento.

Many books and literature of the period spoke despairingly of tenderfoot behavior and documented its negative results. The works of Willa Cather and Laura Ingalls Wilder were two politically disparate authors that went into great detail regarding the life of the prairie family and the unusual harshness of the people brought up in its culture. Death and injury was often the result of showing weakness or kindness to those less fortunate or less able to fend for themselves.

In Willa Cather's *O Pioneers!* – 1913, the young lovers Marie and Emil discover an illicit love together and are caught later beneath a tree by her husband Frank Shabata who shoots them both for their infidelity. Shabata is used in the book to show the wild irrationality and anger exhibited by powerful men in prairie life with his redemption for his actions coming in the form of a harsh prison term. What is important about the novel is its intricate description of the unrelenting brutality of pioneer life, and its extensive homage to the severe personality traits of early pioneers.

Cather's work has often been corrupted and hijacked by the leftist movement as a criticism of American pioneer life, declaring Cather a lesbian (due to her numerous personal female friendships) and her works a promotion of "queer theory"[60] and that the net effect of rugged individualism was that of destitution, despair and death.

---

[60] Queer theory is a field of critical theory that emerged in the early 1990s out of the fields of LGBT studies and feminist studies. It is a kind of interpretation devoted to queer readings of texts.

The scholar Janet Sharistanian who did much background on Cather's work said:

Cather did not label herself a lesbian nor would she wish us to do so, and we do not know whether her relationships with women were sexual. In any case, it is anachronistic to assume that if Cather's historical context had been different, she would have chosen to write overtly about homoerotic love." (*Introduction to My Ántonia*, New York: Oxford University Press, 2006)

Cather destroyed most of her own personal letters and writings and so there is much speculation about her private life, but Sharistanian is absolutely correct in her assessment of Cather's work. The issue of Cather's sexuality is irrelevant regarding the content and descriptive nature of her work on the people of that period. The descriptions, style and analysis of the American pioneer is sexually neutral in context, especially considering the characters were fictional. Although her stories and works revolved around romance, they are nevertheless descriptive of the harshness of pioneer life, and not a critique on the appropriateness or politics of such a way of life--merely a good romantic story. The central issue of her work was not of blame or accusation but that of documentation as the backdrop of a romance story. The element of the difficulties of pioneer life, while well documented in Cather's work, were used not to promote a political agenda but rather to provide context and texture to her essentially romantic stories. The characters' of Cather's novels were not the net result of the harsh pioneer life, but instead were individuals struggling to deal with the harshness of life in the prairie and in that sense were a study in the nobility of man in an untenable situation.

To put things in perspective, take the example of Laura Ingalls Wilder, whose collection of *Little House on the Prairie* (1932-1943) books went into marvelously readable descriptions of life in the mid-1800's. While the television show (starring Michael Landon) popularized the novels; it bore little resemblance to Wilder's actual novels. Even though geared for a youth reader, the key to the books was that these were not fictional characters but real people and an almost professional historical description of the pioneer mentality. Wilder's stories came from recollections of her own childhood, and stories about her own father and family and the brutality and random harshness of Miswest pioneering life.

In her books she documented her father Charles' absolute single minded pursuit of escaping civilization and government at almost all costs to his family. And yet through the series, Charles Ingalls has an intense love for his family for which he risks life and limb almost daily to protect. Charles Ingalls was not unique. The majority of people that settled the West and expanded the frontier did so for the same reasons as Charles Ingalls. They would rather risk their life and family than live under a protective and intrusive government.

This dichotomy of risking his family and yet at the same time risking himself to protect them in that environment is emblematic of the pioneers of this period. To them the dangers of an expansive and protective government were far greater than the risk of death, illness or disability from living on the prairie. As a result, such a way of life also become iconic of American Exceptionalism.

In one spectacular case Ingalls was faced with starvation from a poor seasonal crop. He made the decision to work in a neighboring town while his family ground up individual grains of wheat to chew on until he returned. What was remarkable about the account was that the "neighboring town" was over forty miles away--a trek he made on foot several times a month to bring food and money to his starving family--all of which he bore without complaint. There are few people today that would make such a sacrifice for their families in a society where people demand payments deposited directly to their accounts from the government to make sure their cell phone does not get turned off. The concepts of unemployment payments and monthly mortgage payments for land that would have exceeded Ingalls' annual salary, or food stamp programs feeding millions of people would have made him ill with the horror of an all-encompassing and overpowering government as its price.

Ingalls would have seen that sort of lifestyle as one of weak ennui, and a nation of tenderfeet. His family lived on food that would have sickened a Billy goat, and they lived that way as a matter of choice, not by force of unemployment or circumstance. This was the true power of pioneer life that these men and women by literally the tens of thousands *chose* to live this way to avoid the risk of government oversight and to make sure their children and their children's children lived free of oppression and under a flag woven by liberty, and not by oversight.

This is the key element, the issue of personal choice in a life that was decidedly harsh. The Ingalls family moved west and into these sorts of difficult lives by choice, not by natural forces such as economic changes. Paid work was plentiful back east, but with that work came the costs of government controls and the lack of opportunity for both wealth and personal freedoms.

Later on in life, Laura Wilder (name by marriage) wrote these books while at the same time building a large empire of farms and fruit orchards built by years of relentless hard work tending to the lands she and her family had settled. Even more impressive, the Wilders lost most of their lands and fortune in the Great Depression and crash of 1929, a fact not mentioned in her books since she had stopped writing in 1930 even though the *Little House* books did not reach publication until 1932 at the earliest. She paid off her debts by selling her lands, and she was left with approximately 200 acres. While the royalties of her books published from 1932 onward kept her and her husband, who was crippled from diphtheria and polio, living a comfortable life on what was left of her farms, Wilder never was a wealthy woman. Her books sold well into her later years and her death in 1957 at the age of 90 left only small estate to her now vast family.

When asked about her books and why she wrote them, her humble pioneer background was apparent--she once said the reason she wrote her books in the first place was to preserve the stories of her childhood for today's children, and to help them to understand how much America had changed during her lifetime and not for personal gain or wealth. This is why the books were written in a "youth format" which made them easily readable and simple to understand. She also converted the books to a more "adult" format with the help of her daughter Rose Wilder Lane in the novels *Let the Hurricane Roar* (1932) and *Freeland* (1938).

Rose Wilder Lane's involvement with her mother's pioneer life and her authorship of the *Little House* series did not end with her literary work. Together from 1930 or so onward, they became leaders of the now growing libertarian movement that was picking up speed in Roosevelt-era America. They often spoke at many club meetings and town hall meetings to audiences that resented the increasing influence of the federal government in the everyday lives of people living in the Midwest.

Ayn Rand described Wilder and Lane as the "founding mothers" of the American libertarian movement and strong proponents of the antiracism movement that was building momentum in the eastern cities.[61] Lane continued the literary genius of her mother's work well into the 1940's and 1950's working in numerous libertarian and anti-communist

---

[61] In 2009, New Yorker writer Judith Thurman recounted how Laura and Rose both became successful writers, and "crabby collaborators" and critics of the New Deal. As Thurman wrote The New Yorker, Rose Wilder Lane is considered with Ayn Rand and Isabel Paterson "a founding mother" of libertarianism. She left her estate and the rights to the "*Little House*" books to her close friend, Roger Lea MacBride, a Libertarian Party candidate for president in 1976.

movements until her death in 1968. She was the first author to coin the term "libertarian" to promote the rugged individualistic lifestyle now fading in the twilight of civilization and in the expansionist government under Franklin Delano Roosevelt. As late as 1965 she had toured Vietnam to do an amazing and widely heralded magazine series touting the importance of American individualism over the rise of Communism in Southeast Asia.

Libertarianism and its cousin conservatism were essentially built and focused upon both equal rights for women and minorities during this period. The Wilder's worked tirelessly for both causes and tied the two irrevocably together, at least until modern day times when Democrats and leftist tried to portray conservative movements as racially biased and opposing equal rights. The Democrats successfully co-opted the libertarian based anti-racism movement by creating the concept of government sponsored programs like Affirmative Action and other social constructs which were not the intent of the original anti-racism libertarian movement. Most of these constructs were originally designed to 'promote' people of color, which did much to change the Democrat party from the party of slave-owner south to the modern ideas of liberalism and Progressive thought. The days of Wallace standing on the courthouse steps ended with the politics of Johnson and Kennedy, but were no less racially biased in nature—certainly in comparison to libertarian ideals of one people, one law, and one vote.

All of that and considerably more, were major contributions to libertarianism and American Exceptionalism, and all are the direct result of Charles Ingalls and pioneers like him, who refused to become the servants of an expanding government in 1850's prairie America. The story of Charles Ingalls and others like him are portraits in American courage and emphasize the value of a single person's contribution to society, even if by the fact that it was his daughter and granddaughter that brought his life into the light of public opinion. One has to wonder at the net result of American freedom and rugged individualism of the Midwest pioneers-- would they have failed or not been the men and women of fortitude they were, would European dictators and theories like Nazism and Fascism have succeeded? Would their children have had the grit to fight these ideas or travel to those lands and stopped them in their tracks?

The theory of living in harshness and difficulty building the character of the American persona is typified and romanticized in many novels but is nevertheless apparent in the actions of American society in the events leading up to what has been described as the "greatest generation"--the men and women who fought in World War II. Had America not fought its way through the settlement of the West and adopted a self-sufficient lifestyle in the late 1890's through the 1930's, the people of the United States might not have had the fortitude to either fight or win the Second World War.

The generations of Americans that fought in World War One and Two were called the "greatest generation" and not without cause.[62] NBC journalist Tom Brokaw wrote in his 1998 book *The Greatest Generation* writes:

My father, Red Brokaw, was a blue-ribbon member of that fix-it generation. My mother learned not to say aloud what she needed, say a new ironing board, because my father would immediately build her one. She liked to buy something from the store occasionally. When I was a young man in need of spending money I mentioned that I could mow many more lawns if I had a power mower. I had a snazzy new model from Sears Roebuck in mind. My father went to his workshop and built a mower using an old washing machine motor, welded pipes for handles, a hand-tooled blade, and discarded toy wagon wheels mounted on plywood platform. He painted it all black and it was a formidable machine. At first I was embarrassed, but then as it drew admirers I was proud of its homespun place in a store-bought world.

The generation that fought these wars had learned the lessons of their prairie parents and grandparents, that hard work and ingenuity were the tools of success, not reliance on government nor on the help from neighbors. While the modern conveniences' of refrigeration, industrialization and progress were welcome, they did not reject the notion of hard work being key to that success, but instead embraced it. And all of it simply because individuals had the fortitude to say "no" to government. This is the power of individual rights and why we, as Americans, must act similarly today.

---

[62] The 'greatest generation' was a term coined by NBC correspondent Tom Brokaw

Buffered by her two great oceans to the east and west, America had become involved in World War One only after great debate and much planning. It also was a late entrant to the war, using its vast material and manpower needed to break the stalemate on the Western front. To say that it wished to stay out of World War Two was more than a mild understatement. Congress was almost rabid about it in 1935. England and France were petrified of the prospect of another war on their borders, and by 1935 they were caving in to more and more German demands in order to provide peace at all costs, and America was passing new and more stringent neutrality acts on an almost daily basis. President Roosevelt knew the eventual outcome would be war with Germany, and he attempted to supply the English and the French with materials and supplies, but he was hamstrung by Congress on numerous occasions. The rise of Hitler in Germany would not be forestalled, and by 1940 war had spread across Europe. In December of 1941 America's hand was forced at Pearl Harbor.

Most of the world still viewed America as a nation of pacifists, country bumpkins and farmers in 1941, but these were the children and grandchildren of the 1900's pioneers and had been hardened by the severity of the Great Depression. Taken as weak and ineffectual by the Japanese, they were instead men and women of deep self-reliance and fortitude--something that went unforeseen by the military planners of the Axis. Most of the enemies of the United States of World War II pointed to the American partying in the "Roaring 20's" and the subsequent rescue by government programs as fat and lazy. Roosevelt's own New Deal policies were viewed with derision by most of these then hostile governments. They did not count on the inherent strength of American individualism, nor were they knowledgeable about America's deep cultural roots of self-sufficiency since they had been masked by programs like Social Security and other New Deal programs. However, the strength, virility and severity of the American military response was amazingly swift and just 18 months later in 1942 the tide of the war in the Pacific had turned, and the Allies were planning a massive invasion of Europe bolstered by the explosive industrial growth of wartime America.

The concepts of the New Deal and its failed attempt at rescuing the American economy through entitlements and government works projects were quickly eclipsed by the expansion and overwhelming need for manpower not only in factories but on the battlefield. The pioneer women of the libertarian movement soon found themselves pounding rivets in the factories while the men marched off to destroy the consummate evil of the Nazis and the militaristic imperialism of the Japanese empire. This was entirely missed by the hostile Axis powers who were forced to rely on slave and forced labor to achieve the same armaments that were being built by the millions of free individuals in the States who were far more productive and innovative than the Nazis who were merely masters of a team of men under the crack of the whip.

While FDR was President from 1932 to 1939 there was virtually no growth and little Gross Domestic Product (GDP) expansion under the myriad of government works projects of the New Deal. GDP growth averaged less than one percent per year during that entire period. By 1945 the United States GDP growth was now in the double digits and America's poverty stricken and hardship laden years were now behind it. The enormous growth of the GDP from 1939 to 1945 was primarily due to changes in American factory production, not the welfare state Roosevelt had created.

Key to this period was the transition from the pioneer, self-reliant lifestyle of Wilder's Midwest to Franklin Roosevelt's entitlement laden culture of Depression era America. However, with economic growth in the double digits, people forgot about the enormous costs Social Security and economic planning would have once that growth naturally tapered off. Instead Americans enjoyed a quality of life and standard of living that could not be matched by the now largely destroyed Europe. America's nation of pioneers and the thrifty working class that defeated Hitler and Tojo would raise children who knew no hardships as they had and who had grown accustomed to checks in the mail when they got sick or retired. They were now the very thing the pioneering Charles Ingalls and others like him sought to avoid--a nation of tenderfeet reliant upon the succor of an all-powerful government. The roots of the stalwart character built by life on the prairie had rotten branches fed by the overwatering of government dependence and burgeoning growth.

While today it is outrageous that governments and society must be forced to choose between which group of people to aid due to low balances in the treasury from overspending, it is even more outrageous that our society must rely upon the government for its subsistence, at least as far as the pioneer mentality is concerned.

With federal and state payrolls at an all-time high, and treasury balances at an all-time low, the question remains whether or not the current US government can continue to support essentially a nation of tenderfeet. The obvious answer to the uninformed would be to simply raise taxes but with the people in such dire need of every dollar and deficits so high, simple mathematics precludes the raising of taxes to solve the problem.

The worst part is that people in need now have the *expectation* that government should bail them out, that the government is the answer to economic woes and poor life decisions and that misfortune is mainly a taxpayer problem not the individuals. The uniquely American experience of individual liberty and self-reliance which created the largest period of national growth from 1860-1920 has gone by the wayside in exchange for the comfort and government dependence of 2011. What has been lost is the understanding that poverty, illness and life troubles are not the cause of government, and thus government should not be blamed if it is unable to provide redress against them. Instead, government is now blamed when it cannot solve these intractable age old problems, or when it cannot provide money as a salve to the wound.

However, America's monumental growth of the Gilded Age built by the hardworking pioneers could not last, and the bills would soon come due from Wilson's and FDR's legacies and the monster entitlements of Johnson and Kennedy for the demanding masses they had created in the late night planning rooms of the White House.

8 THE ONSET OF ENNUI

Employment and ennui are simply incompatible- Dorothy Deluzi

With the increasing growth of entitlements and the notion of entitled government services growing in American culture, it necessarily meant that the monies that are being devoted to entitlements would be no longer available for public works or projects that would not only strengthen the nation's economy and infrastructure but its moral and self-worth as well. If you spend a tax dollar to feed child, that is one less dollar that is available to build a bridge, repair a pothole in an broken road, or in the pocket for the taxpayer to spend.

The ancient civilizations of Rome and Greece, as well as Renaissance Europe, knew well the importance of societal public works that could stand the test of time and would be emblematic of a culture even long after it was gone. The Great Pyramids of Egypt, the Sistine Chapel, the Coliseum--these are all great public infrastructure projects funded by governments in order to provide not only a service to the people but as a lasting monument to their culture as well. These monuments became a center of civilization, a source of pride to the people, and a reminder to the heirs of the builders of the importance of that period of time.

However, the longer a monument is built to last, the more maintenance it requires and necessarily means as entitlements increase, so does the margin narrow for those repairs to take place.

Until the turn of the century and the rise of American power after World War I and World War II, the United States had little to show future civilizations in the way of grand public works. Teddy Roosevelt's Panama Canal was the first modern marvel of the world, but it was situated in another country. It was too remote to provide the societal boost that such a feat would normally provide. Later on, Franklin Delano Roosevelt's public works projects of the Hoover Dam, while enormous, were ultimately meant for providing power and supply to a growing nation and not monuments to success as the Pyramids were. These were not monuments to public infrastructure or of lasting importance but of productivity—the hallmark of American success. These were works to keep people employed in times of need as well. In time, projects like the Panama Canal and the Hoover Dam would be simply outmoded by the sands of technological innovation and time.

However, most public policy theorists and historians remembered the great projects of the Roman roads system; roads which are still used today by the peoples of Europe. The logistical changes of a modernized road system would not only be a source of pride to the American people, the vast increase to infrastructure would provide benefits to trade and communication that might last hundreds, if not thousands, of years.

When Dwight Eisenhower assumed the Presidency in post-World War II America, he brought with him an extensive background in logistics and experience of a classical education. Eisenhower was a Mennonite by birth and later on, after his admission to West Point, a Presbyterian by choice. Eisenhower's traditional rugged individualist Midwest background combined with a classical military West Point education, made him an ideal choice to rise quickly through the ranks of the US Army. Serving as an adjunct to MacArthur and General "Blackjack" Pershing, Eisenhower was well versed in the handling of logistical operations and experienced in dealing with the significant problems of the transport and delivery of troops and materiel to the front lines of battle. Eventually becoming the architect of the Allied military victory in Europe over the Nazis, as well as the reconstruction of the now destroyed European economy. He became President of the United States in 1952 when America was reaching the zenith of its economic and military power.

One of Eisenhower's earliest experiences in logistics came in the in-between years of World War I and World War II. Serving as a logistics supply officer he had to take a convoy of troops and arms from coast to coast in 1919 as part of a transcontinental motor convoy. Later on in his memoirs, Eisenhower described the journey as one of the most tortuous of his life, taking months to travel through various back roads and muddy bogs where they would get stuck for days, or get lost in the open and unmarked deserts of the American Southwest.[63]

---

[63] "The Interstate Highway System". Eisenhower Presidential Center. 2008

Later on as he marched armies across Europe, he noticed one advantage the Germans had was the marvelous highways or "autobahns," they had built across the German lands allowing the Nazis to move goods and troops easily to the front from factories well behind enemy lines. Eisenhower felt that America needed such a system too, especially considering the vast size of America, and how the nation had developed over time, essentially by railroad water stops across vast tracts of open land.

As President , Eisenhower he had the ability to change the American infrastructure in a dramatic way, and so he pushed forward the idea of a Transcontinental Highway System, and in 1956, with help from the automotive industry, Congress passed the Interstate Highway Act which would provide funding for the greatest public works project since the Panama Canal, and the largest continuous concrete structure in human history.

The original cost estimates of the system was approximately 25 billion dollars over a 12-year period funded by taxes placed on fuel and diesel oil sales. The actual system was a far greater project, and although technically completed 35 years later at a cost of over 100 billion dollars, the Interstate Highway system is always under repair or construction somewhere in the country today.[64]

Eisenhower pushed the legislation through Congress at considerable political expense to himself, having to go to the

---

[64] The opening of I-70 through Glenwood Canyon in 1992 is often cited as the completion of the originally planned system.

automobile manufacturers for support and lobbying help. In order to get funding and legislation done, Eisenhower convinced Congress that the highway system was critical to national defense, and part of the mandate of the original system was that its central corridors and primary arteries would be determined by the Department of Defense and not local governments or the prurient interests of the automobile manufacturers. This was intended to circumvent the normal political interests of individual Congressman, and promote an efficient and cost effective system. Had Congress been allowed to determine routes, as was originally planned and fought for, many roads would have been put in places that served the prurient interests of individual districts rather than the nation as a whole.

The American interstate system is more than a marvel of construction engineering, it also is a lesson in logistical planning and expertise. The numberings system used was developed by the government where every number of each highway was assigned based on location and direction. Even numbered highways ran east to west, while odd numbers ran north to south. Single digits were international freeways, double were intercontinental and triple were designated as state or local causeways. The numbers started from left to right across the map. Thus, Highway 5 was an international freeway on the west coast while I-95 was an interstate freeway on the East Coast. Some exceptions existed for highways that were already placed, but by and large the highway system allowed easy understanding and location finding even if stuck without a map. The system was designed with military precision and planning, not political one-upsmanship and design by committee.

To say that Eisenhower's Interstate system changed the way Americans lived their lives and the way our country grew would be more than an understatement. Comprising nearly 50,000 miles of continuous roads (not counting state roads), the American system of freeways transports virtually 99% of all the goods sold in the United States and a third of all passenger auto trips use the system at some point.[65]

The American freeway system dwarfs that of any other nation, Germany included, and its annual cost of maintenance exceeds the annual GDP of most other nations. Ninety-three percent of its funding comes from the federal fuel tax, and by law it is mandated to have free and open access along its entire length with exceptions made for some state run toll causeways and highway metering to prevent congestion during busy hours. As such, it represents a major part of American life and productivity.

Revisionist historians look back on the highway system as being a product of the automotive industry interference and lobbying in Congress, but the reverse is true--it was Eisenhower that asked the automotive industry to contribute their expertise and knowledge to the construction and development of the system, and it was Eisenhower that selected then General Motors (GM) president Charles Erwin Wilson as his Secretary of Defense in 1953 well before the

---

[65] "Interstate FAQ". Federal Highway Administration. 2006.

interstate system bill was written. More importantly, as early as 1938, President Roosevelt had developed the embryonic idea of building a national highway corridor coast to coast well before the modern automotive industry was an influence in government. Roosevelt's "Yellow Book" of roads, written in 1939 and completed by 1944 was the basic plan for Eisenhower's interstate system, not anything out of a GM boardroom. This plan was developed by the Director of Public roads, Thomas Herbert, under direction of Roosevelt as a possible extension of the New Deal plans of government works (such as the Tennessee Valley Authority and Hoover Dam) to create jobs and increase employment in Depression era America. While the automobile industries' influence was important and considerable by the 1950's, it was at government's bidding, not the other way around.

Today the interstate system is under attack from a variety of sources, some claiming it contributes to congestion and pollution, others claiming it is in disrepair and too expensive to maintain. Both arguments are ignorant to its essential purpose and its intricate connection to the American economy. The argument ignores the enormous contribution the freeway system has provided to American growth and its daily contribution to the American economy as a whole.

Part of the problem of maintaining the current freeway system is that its overall roadworthiness is still far superior to that of any other roadway system in the world. At 50,000 miles, every mile of it is essentially in serviceable condition; whereas the next nation in line, Germany, has only about 8,000 miles of roadway, with only about 95% of it in serviceable condition.[66] In most countries the navigable major roadways are often completely impassible due to disrepair or local weather conditions. But if there is an issue with the maintenance of the federal interstate system, a modern American wonder, it is one of its own making.

As stated earlier, the construction and early maintenance of the system was funded by the federal fuel tax. At the time of its construction and for the first 12 years, 97% of the fuel taxes in the nation were solely devoted to its construction and maintenance. Today less than 63% of that tax is now going to the system. The other 36% has now been devoted to other projects, such as city rail systems, light rail, bussing and other forms of public transportation which are neither as efficient nor as essential to the American economy.[67] Currently the roads and fuel tax is approximately 18 cents on the gallon. The federal fuel tax was originally designed specifically for the maintenance of the interstate highway system. Furthermore, in other countries where the fuel tax is higher, fuel tax monies are placed to the general fund, as opposed to the US system where the money must be designated for transportation costs--but those transportation costs include anything that involves the Department of Transportation, not the actual roads themselves. As a result, the American system of highways has been morphed into a hodgepodge of different systems around the originally intended universal national transportation corridors. This only serves the local interests of politicians and special interest

---

[66] According to the International Roads and Motorists' Association, 2008 report.

[67] US Office of Management and Budgeting, 2009

groups and are not nearly as efficient. Some of these Department of Transportation pet projects include a University of Hawaii Community College administered driver education program for motorcycle and motor scooter operators, Diversity Sensitivity Training for Department of Transportation employees, Gay/Lesbian outreach programs, Multicultural Awareness seminars, and Tolerance in the Workplace conferences. All of these projects are devoted to creating and protecting the bureaucracy, rather than the original purpose--the maintenance and upgrading of roads and infrastructure.

In 2005 the US Congress under the direction of then Speaker Nancy Pelosi and Senate leader Harry Reid passed HR Bill 3 which devoted federal fuel tax money to small pet projects and was tacked onto a much needed spending bill to ensure its passage. HR 3 diverted over 23 billion dollars of the 41 billion dollar highway fund, more than 50% of the fund,[68] to programs like the Safe Routes to Schools program designed "to enable and encourage children, including those with disabilities, to walk and bicycle to school. . . encouraging a healthy and active lifestyle from an early age." A new Transit in the Parks program would be also be established "to improve visitor mobility and enjoyment" inside national parks. Included in that bill were:

- $3,000,000 to renovate and expand the National Packard Museum;

---

[68] Official US Congressional Record Aug 10, 2005: HR 3 Became Public Law No: 109-59.

- $3,000,000 for the National Infantry Museum Transportation Network;
- $1,705,000 to reconstruct Union Station in North Canaan, Connecticut and establish a transportation museum;
- $1,000,000 to construct the Transportation and Heritage Museum in Townsend, Tennessee;
- $500,000 to Rehabilitate and Redesign the Erie Canal Museum in Syracuse, NY and
- $250,000 for the Issaquah Valley Trolley Project

This diverting of funds actually started in the late 1970's under Jimmy Carter when America began taking the federal fuel tax and channeling it into various entitlement and environmental programs. The federal fuel tax had been scheduled to gradually reduce after completion of the system, but Congress in 1977 deferred the reduction of the tax in an effort to divert funding to fuel and environmental waste cleanup projects which were largely created by private companies. A 2006 report to Congress by the Government and Finance Division detailed the problems of the diversion of funds from federal fuel taxes into other projects instead of the national highway system. The report contends by 1990 the government was forced to increase the fuel taxes to continue to pay for the highways because the revenues from the federal fuel tax had been diverted with greater frequency to pet projects of special interest groups including increasing taxes on non-highway use fuels such as stove, heating and camping fuels.

One of the biggest single diversions of the federal fuel tax that resulted in large increases in 1994-97 under Clinton, was to interstate and local rail and light railway systems. The intent was to promote the use of high speed and interstate railways systems in the US over the primary design of the interstate highways system. Thus the fuel tax designed to maintain the interstate highway system was being used against itself for the political ideologies of the left wing of American politics. Billions of much needed maintenance dollars were being diverted away for entitlement projects to support the political agenda of politicians and union interests.

While the interstate system of highways is all connected and contiguous, the bulk of the rail and light rail systems in America are not, and they are incompatible with each other. Furthermore, the distance between cities in America is nearly three times as far as Europe and largely decentralized. Interlinking rail systems in the US would be neither efficient nor viable from a sheer logistical point of view, despite the desire to mimic Europe's high speed rail lines. Most importantly they could never be used for the original intent of the interstate system--the large scale movement of populations and troops in the event of war or natural disaster.

In short, the concept of adding high speed rails, or using rail lines in the US for mass transportation would be overly expensive, inefficient and counterproductive to an already marvelously simple and efficient system. It would be re-inventing the wheel.

The restructuring of the federal fuel tax has inadvertently led to a restructuring of the national transport system with the typical deleterious effects of a lack of coordination, competition of interests, and low maintenance standards. Had the US kept the tax solely devoted to the development and maintenance of the highway system, it would be far more modernized, efficient and in much better shape than it currently is today—despite it being the envy of the world. Argument could also be made that federal fuel taxes could even have been lowered by now and still had better end results.

While the Chinese system of interstate highways, the National Trunk Highway System (NTHS), is quickly approaching that of the size of the American system (approximately 40,000 miles as of this printing), it is almost entirely built as a toll road system with only limited public access, and despite its massive expenditures on construction, it is primarily a privately owned system with private corporations operating them on a for profit basis. Interestingly a number of attempts to assess a fuel tax on the people of China to own and maintain the roads has been largely met with protests and ridicule. As such the Chinese government has been unable to control or seize ownership of the highways, much to the government's chagrin.

Shockingly though, and a thumb in the eye of big government types, the NHTS is a sole standout in quality and efficiency in comparison to Chinese rail and other transportation systems. Its roads use a similar system of numbering and lettering to the American freeway system, and they tend to be well-lit, non-congested and easy to use. Private industry in China has done a marvelous job of fashioning its highway system after the American concept of interstate highways and is in many ways a duplicate of Eisenhower's system.

While American political interests point to the benefits that other countries (particularly China) attain using transportation methods such as high speed trains and other public transportation methods, it is the Chinese NTHS, a privately and independently run highway system, that is the fastest expanding transportation system in the world--built with public dollars in partnership with industry, but maintained and run by private companies.[69]

In comparison, the much lauded Chinese high speed rail system, which America is now trying to reinvent as its own national transportation system (to theoretically replace our freeway system), only handles less than a million passengers in a national population five times that of America. Chinese high speed rail travels from city to city by largely empty trains; the average train leaves a station with less than 25% of capacity. Critics in China contend that the government's design, construction and promotion of the high speed rail system was not one of a genuine desire to improve transportation, but to put a dent in the private companies

---

[69] China Expressway System to Exceed US Interstates, newgeography.com, Feb 10, 2011

that own the NHTS and thereby drive them into bankruptcy, and take over the highways system and its profits.[70] Ticket prices for high speed rail in China are very expensive and it uses massive amounts of energy, five times that of an ordinary diesel train and 10 times the energy cost of an automobile using a highway system. Almost every high speed rail line, not only in China but elsewhere, is a losing proposition financially. China has spent hundreds of billions of dollars on its high speed rails, with little hope of recovering its losses and no end in sight to its capital outlays for annual maintenance and repair. The Minister of Rails in China announced in 2010 that it would be forced to lower the speed of all the rail lines below 190 miles per hour due to safety and cost concerns, thus eliminating the inherent advantage of timeliness over other more efficient forms of transportation. China has declared high speed rail lines as a replacement for highways or other forms of transportation largely unsustainable and by 2014 they expect the entire system to fail under bankruptcy[71]. As of 2011 the current company running the high speed rail lines for China is being investigated for massive fraud and government bribery, a crime in China that is punishable by death.[72]

---

[70] Wang, Chongxu; Yuancheng Peng, Yinbo Liu (January 2009). "Crossing the Limits". Civil Engineering (Reston, Virginia: American Society of Civil Engineers)

[71] China Rail Ministry 'Kingdom' May Be Split Up on Fatal Crash
Posted in China, China Corruption, China Investing, China Transportation on August 4, 2011 by infoseekchina

[72] China's deadliest high-speed train crash may hasten the breakup of a ministry that runs the world's second-largest rail network, employs more people than the US government and has debts larger than Denmark's entire economy. 2011, infoseek.com.

For America to ignore one of the largest and most efficient highway systems in the world in an attempt to reinvent itself as a European style of transportation networks or a Chinese style of railway transportation is a monumental blunder from both an economic and logistical point of view. The Chinese high speed rail system may be an engineering feat, it is a logistical and economic failure with debts greater than the entire economy of Denmark's GDP. While high speed rails have a place in any transportation system, the idea of their ability to replace highways as either a passenger transport system or as the primary transportation method of goods is an idea not backed up by facts, but as it is in China, merely a pretense for a political agenda. It is unreasonable to assume that a high speed rail is either efficient or economical since there is literally zero empirical evidence to go by that suggests it is successful in any nation in the world. The most successful model for increasing the efficiency, productivity and survivability of the American highway system is to simply keep the taxes it derives from its use solely and wholly devoted to its maintenance and upkeep with any excess balance returned to the people from which it was taken-- either by tax reductions or by the restoration and repair of local roads. This was the original intent of the concept of the fuel tax. Other countries have used their fuel taxes as a source of revenue into the general fund with poor results in the design and maintenance of the their respective roads systems. As America shifted to this model of fuel taxation,[73] it

---

[73] The Fund receives hypothocated tax revenues derived from excise taxes on highway motor fuel and truck related taxes on truck tires, sales of trucks and trailers, and heavy vehicle use. Money goes to the general treasury but is then credited to the fund- thus is subject to earmarking.

too has begun to suffer from the same problems other nations have insofar as transportation efficiency.[74]

American know how and engineering skill once again has proven itself as the successful model by which the world is moving forward, and the steps the world has taken in transportation to model itself after America has been an enormous boon to economic growth, much as it was in 1950's America. Countries like France and Spain who moved forward with a public transit and railway system of transportation have fared poorly in comparison. While there are many factors to economic growth in a nation, its transportation system is a massive contributing factor, and where those factors have been hampered by government intervention, such as in China's high speed rail adventure, it has largely been a failure and counterproductive. The American model of its National Highway system is both an economic success and a testament to American society at its height--a monument to the American economy that will stand the test of time.

Sadly, the America interstate system is the last and best monument to American private ingenuity and know-how and marks the beginning of the end of America's shift of its public monies toward entitlements and away from societal progress. As government became more obsessed with changing and reinventing its capitalist and freedom based foundations, America was turning inward and going back toward a societal vision that they had fled from 200 years earlier.

---

[74] Then-Secretary of Transportation Mary Peters stated on August 15, 2007 that about 60% of federal gas taxes are used for highway and bridge construction. The remaining 40% goes to earmarked programs.

With that groupthink came the ennui of failure and the rugged individual nature of American Exceptionalism was beginning to die.

9 COLORBLIND AMERICA

When I was a kid, we said that we were precluded from going to certain neighborhoods because of the color of our skin... Now the neighborhoods are the neighborhoods of ideas, you're not supposed to be there because ... of the color of your skin. — Clarence Thomas

One of the great accusations against the United States is the perceptions that America is a nation based in racism, and to this day that its politics and economy are driven by inherent racist principles and laws. Yet it was by the late 1920's that the human condition of the anti-racism movement began to pick up steam in America and was largely driven by a handful of authors and philosophers who drew from their roots in the pro-individualism movement as a response to the rise of American Progressivism. While modern scholars view conservative and libertarian interests and groups as enablers of racism, it is instead the left and the Progressive Movement in the 1920's that are the foundation and perpetrators of institutionalized racism today. The colored skin people of Africa and South America arrived as slaves in 1700's America, but after their freedom in the Civil War (Emancipation Proclamation, 1863) in less than 100 years were essentially equals under the law in America, leading to the first black President in 2008.

At the time of Great Depression when jobs became scarce and the economy had soured on the robust lifestyle of the "Roaring 20's," the American people started to look inward at themselves as a possible source of their own societal problems. Out of the misery of human poverty and suffering, the power of capitalism and its economic principles began to take a back seat to the theory of Progressivism and government intervention in the lives of every day Americans. Part of that political theory fed on the building resentment of blacks and other minorities' as somehow less deserving and thus "stealing" jobs from "regular" (a.k.a. white) Americans.

A key element of this theory revolved around the notion that some people in society were less productive, and thereby more deserving of government aid or support. Authors and other social scientists began to consider the now scientifically possible theories of advancing human evolution through genetic and social engineering and the controlling of dangerous genetic flaws in society to prevent threats to human existence. Thus the progressive societal models of affirmative action, Planned Parenthood and racial rebalancing (bussing and forced integration) are theories that evolved from the theories of eugenics and genetic cleansing.

The Progressives began to promote the social concept known as "eugenics," or the active role of government in the normal biological development of man. By 1932 promoters of the theory of eugenics had their International Eugenics conference in New York, and the theory of eugenics was taking center stage in the American Progressive Party. Politicians and authors of modern individualism such as Rose

Wilder Lane wrote strong critiques of the Progressive Party's involvement with the eugenics movement, but the movement had strong supporters in its corner such President Woodrow Wilson, John Maynard Keynes and John Harvey Kellogg as well as Major General Frederick Henry Osborn, a philanthropist and military leader.[75] Considering the combined effects of government involvement with Roosevelt's New Deal and the massive collapse of the economy in the Great Depression, the idea of eugenics and the culling of minorities, mental defectives and those with heredity disorders appealed to the masses who were finding it difficult to find even menial jobs. Sensible minds such as Lane and others, understood the racist overtones and implications of modern eugenics but their concerns were largely ignored. The Progressive Party leaned heavily on the combined works of notable social scientists such as Harry Laughlin, who passed and promoted new compulsory sterilization laws, and Margaret Sanger, founder of Planned Parenthood.

Part of the argument for eugenics revolved around the now common practice of animal husbandry (controlled breeding) which was doing wonders for modern farming yields and was making great strides in solving the growing hunger problem in the United States. In theory eugenicists believed that "human husbandry" could solve many of society's great problems such as poverty, sickness, disease and even overall intelligence and social well-being.[76]

---

[75] The American Eugenics Society is an organization started by promoting racial betterment, eugenic health, and genetic education through public lectures, exhibits at county fairs etc., but under the direction of Frederick Osborn, started to place greater focus on issues of population control, genetics and later medical genetics.

The first elements linking racism with eugenics actually arrived in the social consciousness as early as 1894 from three Harvard scientists that promoted the concept of eugenics theory when they sought to legally bar immigrants from Mexico and other Latin American countries from entering the United States.[77] They felt that these people were racially inferior to the "superior stock" of those of northern Anglo-Saxon stock. Working with the American Progressive Party they had succeeded in passing the American Immigration Act of 1924 which barred entry of Hispanic Americans to the United States to protect America from breeding with "socially inferior stock." The Act was repealed in 1952 and rewritten, and is now used to establish immigration quotas into the US by the Department of Immigration.

Tying into the modern Progressive Party's work toward a eugenically cleansed society was their promotion of euthanasia as a method of disposing of the sick and elderly in a humane way. The Illinois Homeopathic Medicine Association lobbied heavily for mass euthanasia laws as a way of dealing with the large amounts of elderly and sick patients clogging their hospitals and sanitariums,[78] mostly as a result

---

[76] A current proponent of animal husbandry is the Food and Agricultural Organization of the United Nations (FAO). From their website: Achieving food security for all is at the heart of FAO's efforts--to make sure people have regular access to enough high-quality food to lead active, healthy lives. FAO's mandate is to raise levels of nutrition, improve agricultural productivity, better the lives of rural populations and contribute to the growth of the world economy

[77] Encyclopedia of North American Immigration 2010.

[78] In 1931, the Illinois Homeopathic Medicine Association began lobbying for the right to euthanize "imbeciles" and other defectives. The Euthanasia Society of America was founded in 1938 : The Black Stork: eugenics and the death of "defective" babies in

of the now dwindling economy, and with the progress of medical techniques the concept of compulsory sterilization became more practical and widely accepted.

Remarkably, eugenicists managed to pass not only compulsory sterilization laws against the sick and deformed but also against many that were simply marked by the fact that they were indigent. By 1931 at least eighteen states had passed compulsory sterilization laws around poverty and racial stereotyping. The most infamous case was one Carrie Buck who sued the government claiming her forced sterilization was due to her poor life and possible mulatto heritage, as well as her limited intelligence, not actual mental infirmity.[79] In *Buck vs. Bell*, the Supreme Court upheld Buck's sterilization in an eight to one vote, and in the quote now made famous, Chief Justice Oliver Wendell Holmes claimed "three generations of imbeciles was enough."[80] In his opinion Holmes wrote:

"We have seen more than once that the public welfare may call upon the best citizens for their lives. It would be strange if it could not call upon those who already sap the strength of the State for these lesser sacrifices, often not felt to be such by those concerned, in order to prevent our being swamped with

American ... By Martin S. Pernick year

[79] Carrie Buck was paroled from the Virginia Colony for Epileptics and Feeble-Minded shortly after she was sterilized. Under the same statute, her mother and three-year old daughter were also sterilized without their consent. Carrie Buck went on to marry William Eagle. They were married for 25 years until his death. Scholars and reporters who visited Buck in the aftermath of the Supreme Court case reported that she appeared to be a woman of normal intelligence.

[80] *Buck v. Bell*, 274 US 200 (1927), was the United States Supreme Court ruling that upheld a statute instituting compulsory sterilization of the unfit, including the mentally retarded, "for the protection and health of the state."

incompetence. It is better for all the world, if instead of waiting to execute degenerate offspring for crime, or to let them starve for their imbecility, society can prevent those who are manifestly unfit from continuing their kind. The principle that sustains compulsory vaccination is broad enough to cover cutting the Fallopian tubes."(1924)

However, the separation of a people by defining those a "defective" and those as normal, led to some spectacularly nasty results in World War II Germany. German law, as well as other European nations, also believed in modern progressive eugenics, and were building new legal and medical laws and codes around these theories. German social scientists and experts looked to the Virginia law case of *Buck vs. Bell* as the prototype for their own change in law. In 1935, a decade after the passage of Virginia's eugenics laws, the Virginia registrar of statistics, Walter Ashby Plecker, who developed the racial criteria behind the act wrote to Walter Gross, director of Nazi Germany's Bureau of Human Betterment and Eugenics. Plecker described Virginia's racial purity laws and requested to be put on Gross' mailing list. Plecker commented upon the Third Reich's sterilization of 600 children in Algeria who were born of German women by black fathers:

"I hope this work is complete and not one has been missed. I sometimes regret that we have not the authority to put some measures in practice in Virginia."[81] (1935)

---

[81] Warren Fiske, "The Black and White World of Ashby Plecker", 2004

Standing against this onslaught of racism and eugenics by the now Progressive Wilson US government, were many black and libertarian authors of the period. The conservative and independent pro-libertarians fought back against these eugenicists arguing that the Constitution protected the rights of all men equally regardless of sex, race or biological background. They rejected the notion of compulsory sterilization and segregation of populations by color or genetic makeup as being anti-American and attempted to pass their own legislation barring eugenics laws and theory. The libertarian author Rose Wilder Lane worked with black authors to form anti-racism and pro-freedom rallies and organizations primarily in the South where the Progressives had their strongest defenders. The roots of modern racism and the element of government controls placed on racial minorities link back to these two schools of thought--the ideal society created by government and the Progressive Movement, versus the libertarian ideal of a free society and the individual deciding their own role in society.

With the collapse of Nazi Germany the world looked on in horror at what a government machine could do given unbridled support of the theories of eugenics and the separation of people defined by race or physical ability rather than standing by the original principles of the American Constitution which held that all people were separate and individual but equal. The Nazi war machine (whose own 1933 Nuremberg Eugenics laws were drafted based off American sterilization laws)[82] had not only perfected the eugenics

---

[82] Mommsen, Hans "The Realization of the Unthinkable: The "Final Solution of the

theory but had institutionalized it as a way of not only biologically cleansing its own people but half of Europe of whomever they denoted as politically or biologically undesirable. The mass extermination of millions of Jews as well other ethnics such as Slavs, Serbians, Gypsies and homosexuals was the end result of the concept of government sponsored eugenics. While the concentration camps of Nazi Germany are an extreme example of organized and governmental sponsored eugenics, it has been proven time and time again such theories devolve into mass exterminations such as the ones seen in modern day countries like the Balkans and African nations.[83] The original theories of promoting the general welfare in pre-1930 Germany were now being used as a tool by an all-powerful government to simply "do away" with the enormous costs of promoting and protecting anyone of ideal physical selection.

While the original German laws regarding sterilization and segregation (and even the Nuremburg Laws) were originally patterned after American eugenics laws and intended to protect society as a whole from the costs and horrors of disabling genetic illnesses, these social progressive laws eventually became a tool of the Nazi government to simply "dispose" of their problem. The genuine concern and capital outlays of protecting their disabled, their ill and their

Jewish Question" in the Third Reich

[83] In 2001 the International Criminal Tribunal for the Former Yugoslavia (ICTY) found General Krstić guilty of genocide for his role in the 1995 Srebrenica Genocide, thereby making it the first ever legally determined act of genocide by an international tribunal. The International Criminal Tribunal for Rwanda (ICTR) was formed to judge those people responsible for the acts of genocide and other serious violations of the international law performed in the territory of Rwanda, or by Rwandan citizens in nearby states, between January 1 and December 31, 1994.

elderly were being turned inward and the medical camps of 1930 were now simply rows of ovens and experimental labs for sadistic Nazi doctors. Unethical experiments were performed by physicians in these camps on the mentally ill, the disabled and other "undesirables" supposedly in the name of science but served little purpose other than to titillate the growing evil in Berlin. They justified these experiments claiming that these sorts of separate groups of people were somehow different or distinct from the normal Aryan ideal, and that gaining further knowledge into their condition would somehow lead to new discoveries to prevent such illnesses.

Of course, nothing could be further from the truth. The Nazis were murdering mass populations, and entire segments of society were simply done away with under the Progressive argument of eugenics and protecting society from undesirables. The Aryan ideal of blonde, blue eyed and well-muscled adults make the extermination of darker and smaller Jews, Slavs and Hungarians easy under Progressive laws and legal protections.

After World War II modern progressive politics and eugenics theory was looked at entirely differently once the end result was examined. Blacks and other minorities fought side by side with white Americans during the war, and while questionable policies of the Army and Air Force have now been brought to light, this equanimity within the ranks of the armed forces was now becoming more entrenched in American society with the return of the troops. There were few racists in the foxholes of 1940's France.

This shift in political theory from segregation based eugenics theory to modern egalitarianism was remarkably swift in American society from the period of 1940-1960 and was far more swift than what was being seen overseas during this period. American pride revolved around the fact that all Americans were equal under the law, and the theory of the American "melting pot" began to take hold in earnest in American society. Learning from their mistakes in the 1920's and 1930's which directly and indirectly led to the horrors of Nazi Germany, most American courts struck down progressive eugenics laws, and repealed most if not all of them.[84] Nevertheless, most other nations who had similar progressive eugenics laws still felt the need to "protect" mental and genetically deficient people and left many of these on their books--particularly in nations where government provides sponsored medical care or socialized medicine. These nations state the need of such laws to prevent an onslaught of unending medical claims from overwhelming the system. Even our own forays into socialized medicine such as the new Obamacare guidelines will reintroduce such Progressive laws back into American medicine and culture in order to control costs and ration care.

Although the post-war Nuremberg Code was adopted by all western countries to ensure that consent was the first consideration made when using human beings as test subjects in medical and scientific research, there are still many medical laws being maintained which skirt this issue. In Sweden, a

---

[84] On May 2, 2002, Governor Mark R. Warner issued a statement also expressing "profound regret for Virginia's role in the eugenics movement," specifically naming Virginia's 1924 compulsory sterilization laws.

socialized medicine nation, as late as the 1970's some 60,000 people were sterilized, mostly women, in an effort to limit the number of children born with inherited diseases.[85] Europe and the United States still host many institutes for the study of eugenics or "race biology," and these theories are widely publicized in books, lectures and articles. As late as 1972 Alberta, Canada institutionalized men, women and children. After a survivor won a one million dollar lawsuit in 1996, the 700 remaining survivors joined a $700 million class action lawsuit. When the Alberta legislature introduced a bill that would have stripped constitutional protections from the survivors, Canadians were outraged and the province was forced to back down. However, the Alberta legislature limited the compensation to a maximum of $150,000 per victim.[86] China still maintains its own form of eugenics and population control. China introduced new eugenics laws in 1995 which were later renamed the Maternal and Infant Health Laws. The purpose was to prevent inferior births, but the definitions of handicaps and defects were deliberately vague. Enforcement came from local doctors who decided who was "fit" to reproduce and who was not. As the widespread use of socialized medicine increases, so does the risk of returning to eugenics theories and laws designed to cull the population of undesirables. Wiser and cooler heads in America still disavow and fight the notion of eugenics in modern scientific thought but as the enormous costs of maintaining entire populations

---

[85] In these cases consent was given but consent merely meant the issue of having the risk of a defective child was explained to the mentally deficient parent, and since the patient may not have been of mental capacity to make such a decision, the consent was arguably thin. The practice has since been discontinued in Sweden. (faqs.org)

[86] Faqs.org- "On Eugenics"

of genetically ill grow in American society with increased government medical care, it remains to be seen if this line of thought remains.

The speed at which minorities, in particular blacks, began to assert their rights and become interwoven in the American tapestry was remarkably fast by historical comparison to other societal issues. In 1920 blacks were not only segregated but they were an entire social class unto themselves having been freed from slavery for nearly 60 years at that point. By the 1960's, although still subject to racism, blacks were now business holders, Supreme Court judges and an integral part of American social structuring. As a result of this speed, particularly in the South, violence and racial tensions began to explode in cities across America. Rioting and violent protests gave birth to racist organizations such as the Ku Klux Klan and the Black Panthers. But had America not gone through this period of swift social upheaval, it is entirely possible America would still be cursed with a segregated and racially biased society. Most other nations are achieving racial equality in a much slower and more governed manner, and so have not been subject to such widespread violence. Whether or not this is better for society as whole is arguable, but the important fact to understand that is racial violence in America is not a result of underlying racism but instead a product of the *swift* nature of change in American society. Although America was now moving quickly away from progressive separation of the individual groups of cultures and races, and colored races and other minorities still faced an uphill battle to achieve normalization with non-colored people, the change in the American mindset of segregation and discrimination has been profound in less than 60 years.

Other nations also were not as fortunate in this regard. Most other nations, such as those in Europe and Asia, were far more homogenous in skin color and race than was American society. As a result inner city racial tensions, while pronounced in the 1960's, and were largely over by the 1980's,[87] still exist largely intact in nations outside the United States today. South Africa had an official policy such as apartheid (apart-ness) which kept racism in place in a legal social structure as late as 1994. In France it is still illegal to calculate or tabulate statistics based on the color of one's skin, and thus we cannot know to what extent racism plays a role in French society. Chinese authorities use ethnic cleansing and racism as government policy as do many other nations less civilized than the United States. Abhorrent policies of racial murders and crimes, which would not even be conceived of in the modern American legal code or society, are routine in countries like China, India and Southeast Asia. These nations comprise nearly two thirds of the world's population, another fact not mentioned in most leftist arguments about the nature of racism in the world today. Nations with huge populations are viewed as a singular unit but are unfairly compared in this manner to America which has a population less than 10% of these nations. The Balkan nation of Bosnia suffered almost 100,000 deaths as a result of race wars.

---

[87] Inner city rioting and race war related crimes had decreased by over 90% by 1985 per FBI crime statistics. Although "hate crimes" have increased in recent years, that statistic is largely the result of a broadening of the definition of hate crime.

While America is often viewed by other nations as a nation of racist views, it is neither institutionalized as it is in other nations, nor is it as widespread or as virulent as seen in other nations. Other minority groups such as homosexuals are still routinely hung in many countries,[88] and largely peaceful homosexual and transsexual rallies that are held here in the US are often met with beatings and violence in other countries. These facts too are ignored by those that argue that there is an unfair separation of the social choices in society. The use of the word "choices" is deliberate. In American society, any citizen may choose to live their life by any inherent or conscious or unconscious desire whereas in most other nations many such choices are made illegal by law. Homosexuality is an accepted lifestyle in America compared to other countries, and sodomy laws can be found around the world.[89] Today consensual homosexual acts between adults are illegal in about 70 out of the 195 countries of the world (approximately 36%); in 40 of these, only male on male sex is outlawed.[90]

Most importantly, as institutionalized racism is an outlawed practice in American society, it is also considered a major taboo in American culture. Use of pejorative terms and racial epithets is grounds for expulsion from employment and makes an individual a social outcast, as opposed to many

---

[88] Mahmoud Asgari, 16, and Ayaz Marhoni, 18, were Iranian teenagers from the province of Khorasan who were publicly hanged in Edalat (Justice) Square in Mashhad, northeast Iran, on July 19, 2005

[89] While anti-sodomy laws may still be on the books in the US, they are rarely if ever enforced in the case of homosexuality, but used instead in cases of rape or incest.

[90] ILGA World Legal Survey (April 2006)

countries where it is looked at as merely normal human behavior or a societal curiosity. What are also remarkable are the definitive lines of racism being drawn between cultures that would be viewed in America as similar cultures.[91] Take for example the extreme prejudicial difference between Koreans, Japanese and Chinese cultures. In the local environment of Asia and Southeast Asia, these prejudicial lines of racism are profound and definitive, whereas in America, while Asian prejudice exists, these cultures are often lumped together as one in the same. Confusing a Chinese person with a Korean person in America, while insulting, is hardly the crossing of the racial lines that are currently drawn in South Pacific cultures.[92] In short, America and its people have generally rejected the notion of superiority or inferiority based on skin color or heritage, whereas many other nations not only still hold to these beliefs, they maintain such laws and theories as a matter of public interest. The Constitution's specific and careful colorblind definition of one person, one vote and equal protections under the law are the progenitors of all modern anti-racial laws and protections. With the exception of the three-fifths clause (which has been struck and amended from the Constitution) there is no reference to any single race or color in the document.

Take for example India, one of the most populous nations of the world, which officially has rejected its caste system, but still operates in the same manner it has for

---

[91] "More black people jailed in England and Wales proportionally than in US" The Guardian. October 11, 2010

[92] Anti-Korean Sentiment: Seoul, Beijing Should Boost Understanding and Friendship, The Korea Times (Opinion), August 8, 2008

hundreds of years. While racist behavior in America is a societal taboo, it is still a major factor in Indian life and culture. Ads promote skin-bleaching creams that promise to improve one's popularity and career success and boast of light versus dark skin in regards to foreign visas and advanced university degrees. Cultures and religious differences in India often lead to violence and death.[93] Whereas in America there are entire law books devoted to anti-racism laws and rules, there is not a single rule in Indian law books about racial bias or racial protections--only egalitarian protections in place, similar to those found in current American anti-racial rules.[94] With India's 1.1 billion population combined with China's huge numbers, almost 40% of the world's population live in cultures that have no protections for racism or racial bias, and if you factor in the ethnic cleansing nations in Africa and Eastern Europe, almost 70% of the world's population lives in a state of perpetual racial despair; people who not only have to deal with institutionalized racism on a daily basis but have little to no hope of escaping its brutal and offensive edicts. While India has substantial protections in place to reject its formal caste system, its entirely progressive view of its own problems has not improved the living conditions of dark skinned individuals or those of differing religions. The single most factors in improving the life of the everyday Indian has been its shift to capitalism and the ability of Indians to find work in American companies based there. The large influx of

---

[93] A Social History of India, APH Publishing, 2000

[94] In her book *Democracy ana Authoritarianism in South Asia*, Pakistani-American sociologist Ayesha Jalal writes, "As for Hinduism the hierarchical principles of the Brahmanical social order have always been contested from within Hindu society, suggesting that equality has been and continues to be both valued and practiced."

American money vis-à-vis companies hiring and owning factories in India has done more for racial inequality than the progressive and egalitarian affirmative action laws here in America. India has seen its average wage of dark skinned minorities increase dramatically in the last 20 years.[95] American law and culture is far and away less racist and racially biased as other cultures around the globe, and while elements of American racism dwindle daily, they grow by leaps and bound in other countries, particularly in ethnic tribal cultures and countries such as Iran. These parts of the world are not moving forward. They are moving backward from a societal point of view as they cling to backward concepts and Islamic fundamentalist laws. While countries like Iran are attempting to modernize themselves technologically, they are moving forward in a manner that makes their backward thinking more of a threat to world peace and social order than a benefit. It is for this reason, among others, that the American way of life has a beneficial effect on those we trade with and partner with in the development of their nations. The issue that America is a racist and homophobic culture is not only incorrect, it stands in opposition to both our legal code and societal perceptions of minority cultures.

American courts, educational system, and social morays are decidedly anti-racist. However to some, the issue of institutionalized racism is still a viable political activist position, buying power for such societal critics as Jesse Jackson, Al Sharpton and others that garner power from the

---

[95] Friedman, T. (2006). The World is Flat. New York City: Farrar, Staus and Giroux.

issue of racial confrontation. But the argument of societal and institutionalized racism as still a problem in American society is an invalid one, certainly in comparison to other countries that not only legally codify racial policies but accept racial practices in societal order.

America, more than any other nation, has gone to extreme measures to insulate itself from the issue of institutionalized racism, to the point where cases of reverse racism and bigotry have become more commonplace. The case of *Bakke vs. the University of California* brought the issue of reverse discrimination to the forefront of American political thought. Alan Bakke, a 32-year-old veteran of Vietnam with a GPA of 3.51 applied to the University of California Medical School as well as 11 other medical schools. While the majority of the schools rejected his application because of his age, he discovered that although "special applicants" were admitted with significantly lower academic scores than his, the "regular committee often turned down well-qualified minority applicants" claiming that a 3.4 GPA was not a 3.6 GPA-- Bakke's minority status being that of his age, and not his skin color. In 1974 the special admissions committee of UC Davis explicitly stated they would consider only candidates who were from certain minority groups.

The Courts ruled that the special admissions committee was thus practicing "reverse discrimination" against Alan Bakke because of the color of his skin, and the court ordered his admission. He successfully completed his course of study in 1982 and is now a resident physician at the Mayo Clinic in Minnesota. To date, no other country has been documented to have had a similar case as Bakke's, and despite the court ruling and because of the ambiguity of the language of the case, many European schools still use race as a factor in the admission of a student to their curriculum.[96] As late as 2003, while the Supreme Court has affirmed Justice Powell's opinion rejecting "quotas," it still is allowing race to be one "factor" in college admissions to meet the compelling interest of diversity.

The continuation of affirmative action policies of the Progressive Party in modern day America is thereby forcing racism to take on a new mantle in American society. While racism in America is not of the same nature as you might see in foreign countries, it is beginning to resemble that of other nations in the sense that we are not a colorblind society either. The Bakke case is a classic example of this miscarriage of justice. While there are many that would argue that this reverse discrimination is somehow society's version of penance for its acts of slavery in the 1800's, the crimes of slavery were limited in scope (it was typically blacks, not other minorities that were enslaved), and in retrospect, while horrible, were not nearly as severe as the crimes being perpetrated today worldwide. The concepts of institutionalized racism are now directed at non-minority white people in America, and in a circumspect way at "traditional minorities." The legal argument of affirmative action, in principle, contends that a minority cannot succeed in society without government intervention and in doing so marginalizes the abilities of minorities. This argument stands

---

[96] "Admission Policies in Europe" Wihtol De Wenden, Catherine. (1999)

in opposition to Martin Luther King's ideal of a colorblind society:

I have a dream that my four little children will one day live in a nation where they will not be judged by the color of their skin but by the content of their character. (1963)

As America has shifted more to a progressive view of the problems of racism, the condition of minorities in American society is beginning to resemble that of what is happening worldwide. Unemployment and poverty for minorities, particularly African Americans, has increased substantially in recent years,[97] almost in direct relation to the increase of government intervention in racial policy. Graduation rates for minorities have plummeted in inner city locations where government educational rules and standards are at their strongest.[98]

America's move toward an egalitarian sense of justice, as most international cultures have already done, has thus exacerbated the issue of racial imbalances in education and wealth, and the tensions caused by such interference are being exploited daily by those seeking their own aggrandizement and power. Rather than enforcing a colorblind and equal sense of justice, as was originally

---

[97] 16.6% national average according to the Bureau of Labor Statistics, 2011, although better than the close to 3:1 ratio to white unemployment, historically since 1985.

[98] Their unemployment rates in Northern cities were much higher than white unemployment rates in the same cities. One result of black migration to Northern cities was a dramatic increase in the ratio of black unemployment to white unemployment. The black/white unemployment ratio rose from about 1 to 1 in 1930 (indicating equal unemployment rates for blacks and whites) to about 2 to 1 by 1960, and now stands nearly 3 to 1. Source: African Americans in the Twentieth Century- Economic History Association, Feb. 2010

intended in the Constitution, American laws and societal engineering has enforced social egalitarian rules in order to effect social change. The net result has been a consummate failure from a statistical point of view, and an overall destruction of the black family unit.[99] As government promotion of the progressive concepts of "equal but unequal" has increased, and society has stepped away from colorblind equal protections under the law, circumstances for minorities in America have worsened considerably offsetting the myriad gains during the civil rights movement of the 1960's.

A return to an open and libertarian view of the societal issues of discrimination and racism thus is the key to the American way of growth and wealth. The destruction of minority nuclear family units, the lack of good education graduation rates, and the lower pay scales of minorities to whites are all the result of social engineering and leftist government policy making, not any inherent racism in American society. All of these statistics have negatively **increased** in the period following leftist integration of government rules into society. While these rules may have accelerated popular thinking from racial bias to a more integrated society, it has actually sent real progress backwards, since societies now have become more violent and minority cultures relegated into the role of a substandard class. Only through truly equal treatment under the law, as was originally intended, can this be reversed.

---

[99] The 1965 report by Daniel Patrick Moynihan, known as *The Moynihan Report*, examined the link between black poverty and family structure. It hypothesized that the destruction of the black nuclear family structure would hinder further progress toward economic and political equality

Shifting to a colorblind America, rather than one which defines classes of people by the color of their skin would also have a profound effect on the way government jobs and contracts are determined.[100] These costs would directly be passed onto the taxpayer in either the form of reduced taxation or a higher quality of work for the equivalent monies of a more regulated contract. Government websites tout the benefits of affirmative action and color based methods of hiring, but in doing so, government contractors may not be hiring the best and most qualified persons for a job, leading to a commensurate loss in productivity and quality of work. Take for example the case of "Paulette," taken directly from US Department of Labor's website.[101] Paulette is now an Officer of NYNEX, responsible for marketing in Maine, New Hampshire, Rhode Island and Vermont. She says that "Without NYNEX's willingness to actively pursue affirmative action goals, my talents and skills would have never taken me this far in the business world."

This of course, asks a bigger question--is this person qualified or talented enough to perform an adequate job, and if this person has a substandard set of skills, will the employer be able to promote this person further, thus allowing new employees to be hired into her position. If not, a certain sense

---

[100] The US Government imposes a host of socio-economic obligations through its contracts, including requirements related to affirmative action, drug-free work place, subcontracting, and minimum employee wages. Although Congress has streamlined the contracting process to reduce the burdens on contractors offering commercial products and services, any entity considering entering into a government contract must tread carefully.- Federal Government Contract Overview By Carl L. Vacketta of DLA Piper LLP (US)

[101] http://www.dol.gov/ofccp/regs/compliance/aa.htm

of stagnation sets into the position, thus creating the old caste system by defacto--Paulette cannot move up, keeping in the same job year to year, and positions above her go to more qualified candidates. This essentially keeps a person of color or other minority in place with no ability to advance, and perpetuates the glass ceilings that affirmative action was intended to smash. With no incentive nor ability to get the proper skills and talents, employees like Paulette wither on the vine, and are enslaved by the very system that supposedly is protecting them.

Supreme Court justice Clarence Thomas has been an outspoken critic of minority affirming government policies and their inherent costs to society. When Thomas applied to Yale Law School his race was taken into consideration. He wrote in his book:

"I asked Yale to take that fact into account when I applied, not thinking that there might be anything wrong with doing so."

Thomas also says that after he graduated from Yale, he went on several job interviews with "one high-priced lawyer" after another and the attorneys treated him dismissively.

"Many asked pointed questions, unsubtly suggesting that they doubted I was as smart as my grades indicated."

As Thomas indicated in the book as well, that his law degree from Yale was thus "devalued" by affirmative action, and he was humiliated and hurt by affirmative action policies.[102]

In an interview with ABC News, Thomas said he was unable, even when he was nominated to the Supreme Court, to erase the stigmatizing effects of racial preference:

Once it is assumed that everything you do achieve is because of your race, there is no way out...it is irrebuttable {sic] and it is proved to be true. In everything now that someone like me does, there's a backwash into your whole life is because of race."[103]

In short, Thomas indicates that by making society and its growth about racism and affirmative action, rather than about skill sets and abilities, it has devalued the significant contributions of the person of color in America. It is an unfortunate truth that the liberal agenda and leftist thought of the Progressives has insured this same mindset of the slave-owners of the plantation South--that colored people and minorities are a subhuman class that need the aid of the white culture in order to excel and survive. This is the very essence of Progressivism, the inherent discrimination of a society that is not colorblind, and the antithesis of the original Constitution, that all men are created equal under the eyes of God, and protected equally under the law.

This is also the prevailing thought of the non-American cultures worldwide, that the separation of people by culture and skin is necessary in order to promote a political agenda. The concept of multiculturalism[104] over the uniquely

---

[102] *My Grandfather's Son* by Clarence Thomas, 2007

[103] "Silent" Justice Outspoken on Affirmative Action By Ariane de Vogue, Sept. 30, 2007

[104] In a political context it has come to mean the advocacy of extending equitable status

American theory of a melting pot is keeping minorities from truly being equals both under law and via social acceptance.

A rejection of this theory and a return to the idea of one man, one law, one rule and one vote is essential to the long term survival of not only America, but other nations as well. Segregation based on a culture or color or economic hardship or physical disability is never a successful policy, and should not be encouraged either by social acceptance nor fiat of law. While leftists continue to bang the drum for 'multiculturalism' as opposed to the American 'melting pot', in doing so they are returning to the days of segregation and discrimination. There is no such society that is fair and equal If it is a segregated one.

A return to those theories and Progressive policies would restore the separation of the minorities from the majority, the economic stagnation of Civil War South, and make America similar to the casted systems of China, India and Southeast Asia.

But then again, that is what the leftist wants—to be more like our backward European neighbors

---

to distinct ethnic and religious groups without promoting any specific ethnic, religious, and/or cultural community values as central. Multiculturalism as a "cultural mosaic" is often contrasted with the concepts of assimilation and social integration being described as a "salad bowl" rather than a "melting pot."- Dictionary.Reference.com

10 MONROE IN HAND BEATS TWO IN THE BUSH

In the wars of the European powers in matters relating to themselves we have never taken any part, not does it comport with our policy to do so. It is only when our rights are invaded or seriously menaced that we resent injuries or make preparation for our defense. - James Monroe

American foreign policy has always been an enigma to most of the world, and it is probably the primary reason, short of outright jealousy, that Americans are viewed with distaste and in some cases downright hatred, by many people of the world. The primary reason for the vagaries in America foreign policy is that the head of state in America is the President, which is a position that changes every four to eight years, and thus so does America foreign policy to some degree.

While experts point out that American foreign policy has taken great pains to remain consistent over the years, such as the support of Israel and defense of its territorial waters, those consistencies have had varying degrees of shades of grey in their implementation. But central to those shades of grey has been America's obstinate devotion to the protection of its own interests over that of its allies, and up until recently, its central duty to protect the interests of human rights and individual freedoms.

Until the election of James Monroe in 1817, America's interest in foreign policy was simply a matter of expediency over protecting its own borders. The nation had only been formed for about 50 years and the War of 1812[105] was a slap of cold water in the face of most Americans who felt largely isolated from European influence after the British exodus in 1787. Although the war of 1812 ended with an era of good feelings between Britain and the United States, and increased trade and mutual respect, it emphasized America's overall vulnerabilities.

President Monroe, our fifth President, was a remarkably forward thinking leader. He understood that as long as the then-powerful European nations of England, France and Spain had controlling interests and interfered with the development of colonies of the Americas the United States sovereignty could never be assured. Colonization of Latin American

---

[105] The War of 1812 was a military conflict fought between the forces of the United States of America and those of the British Empire. With the defeat of Napoleon in 1814, the British adopted a more aggressive strategy, sending in three large armies with additional patrols. British victory at the Battle of Bladensburg in August 1814 allowed the British to capture and burn Washington, D.C.

countries and its people would forever put a dagger at the throat of American security and thus Monroe, even without a substantial army or navy to argue with, demanded that Latin and South America would be under the protection of the United States and the "Americas would remain for the Americans."

Of course, the policy at the time was met largely with derision and ignored wholesale, primarily because of the United States being unable to defend even her own borders against a serious attack as was shown just years earlier in 1812. Nevertheless, the Monroe Doctrine was respected out of a fear of an American trade boycott not America's military might.

England, which was largely dependent upon American raw materials for import took America seriously but few other nations did at that time. England's stalemate of 1812 also brought with it significant trade benefits and trade rights, and now the island nation was becoming reliant on those imports to fight the war in Europe with Napoleon.

The concept of the Monroe Doctrine, as it came to be known, is the central thesis of American intervention not only in Latin and South America, but that of an overall American policy in the Americas. Many political theorists have argued that the Monroe Doctrine of 1823 is largely defunct now, as Latin and South American nations are now completely independent of their European forbearers and are no longer desire or are in need of protection but modern American Presidents still have encouraged aggressive treatment of

European power in South and Central American spheres of influence.

Contrary to that argument in modern day times has been the heavy influence of Communist interests in post-World War II Latin and South American nations. The European powers of Russia and other Balkan nations invested heavily in the Cuban revolt, as they did in the revolutionary movements of Nicaragua, and Costa Rica in the mid-1980's. As such these nations would pose a serious threat to American security should they become hostile "satellite" nations of enemy powers. They could be used as staging areas for missile attacks, troop launching points or even state sponsored terrorism. Because of this, most American presidents have stuck to the Monroe Doctrine of European non-intervention in the Americas.

Many opponents of American interests have argued vociferously against the Monroe Doctrine as being essentially a pretense for American colonization interests of its own--an argument without merit. To properly examine the charge of modern American colonialism, you have to turn back the clock a bit to the post-World War II 1940's.

At that time America stood as the preeminent world power that had survived the massive casualties and economic damage of Nazi expansionism. Because the United States had defended its shores so vigorously with the Monroe Doctrine up to this point, her oceans had served as a buffer to the violence and agonies suffered by most of the world during this period. The United States was an economic as well as a military powerhouse at this point. England, France, Germany and Japan were virtually decimated to the point of rubble, and Russia's power was largely in her sheer size and numbers. China was still so technologically backward that while it stood as effective counterweight to Russian expansion in the East (due to its enormous population), it could do little to influence world politics.

America had the greatest economic and military advantage worldwide since the Roman Empire's *"pax Romana"* at the turn of the millennium. If South America had been successfully colonized during the 1850's instead of protected by the Monroe Doctrine, Germany would have significant holdings from which to launch attacks on America, not to mention make an invasion of Europe more problematic. German colonization of the Americas were essentially failed attempts to settle Venezuela , the islands of St. Thomas, the Crab Island (Guyana) and Tertholen in the 16th and 17th centuries.   They has also attempted to colonize parts of Chile, Argentina and Brazil, all of which failed to develop once the United States established the Americas as its own protectorate under the Monroe Doctrine.

Yet America did not act upon this significant advantage through conquest or imperial rule. Combined with its sole ability to effectively deliver an atomic weapon to any point on the globe, it could have conquered the world in 1945. No world leader had ever had such a great advantage and NOT used it to conquer or seize territory for its own purpose. If America was going to be a colonizing power, this was the time to do it; nothing would have stood in its way to take large portions of Eastern Europe, Africa or the Asian subcontinent. Only the American concepts of justice, altruism and freedom stood between it and world domination. Significantly it also rode upon the single word of a U. S. President (Franklin Delano Roosevelt and then Truman) to decide the fate of the world through the use of atomic weapons.

This fact is lost upon most leftist historians who seek to reinvent America as a conquering force in modern times. The United States turned over more real estate and territories in the years following World War II than the Germans and Japanese did--almost twice as much when you factor in the lands turned over to the Soviet Union in Eastern Europe and the surrendering of African colonized lands back to the native people for independent status.[106] The lands surrendered by Germany and Japan were not their own lands which were left largely intact (with the notable exception being the Soviet insistence on the division of Germany) despite enormous pressure to dissolve both nations. The nations of Libya, Tunisia and Egypt as independent nations (not to mention Israel) were entirely dependent upon America's withdrawal for their existence. Not only did the Monroe Doctrine protect many lands from colonization by European powers and preserved them for their own people to develop their own nations, it also preserved American security well into the 21st century. In fact, at the end of the war, the United States

---

[106] The Soviet Union took over areas formerly controlled by Germany, Finland, Poland, and Japan. Poland received most of Germany east of the Oder-Neisse line, including the industrial regions of Silesia. Additionally, the Soviet Union had transferred more than 2 million people within their borders from various ethnicities (Germans, Finns, Crimean Tatars, Chechens, etc.)

produced roughly half of the world's industrial output, but by the early 1970's this dominance had lessened significantly

While the Monroe Doctrine is the trunk of the American foreign policy tree, there have been significant additions and variations of the doctrine since 1823. The most significant of which was the Roosevelt Corollary of 1904.

President Theodore Roosevelt modified the doctrine to assert the right of the United States to intervene in Latin America in cases of "flagrant and chronic wrongdoing by a Latin American Nation." Naturally this could be interpreted by many to be American colonialism, but it was done not only to protect the United States from foreign invaders but from foreign covert influence in destabilizing the region. Roosevelt was then able to use military force to aid Columbia, Panama and Cuba from outside influences while they established their own legal governments. Roosevelt did not establish "puppet" governments or American colonies, but instead protected them for their own people--which is unique in this regard. While other nations set up their own controlling governments, such as the British in India, Roosevelt did not. He merely guaranteed their own abilities to be free nations. While critics contend those governments were "friendly" to the US, they certainly were independent of American control and free to govern themselves.

While the use and extensions of the Monroe Doctrine have been a boon of economic prosperity and freedom for the people it protected, the reverse can be said of its abandonment. The ignoring of the Monroe Doctrine and the

Roosevelt Corollary in the Cuban revolution of 1958-59, allowing the Communist dictator to take control of Cuba and not intervening militarily in 1961 (as part of the settlement of the Cuban Missile Crisis) has been costly to the Cuban people on the whole. Cuba's GDP is half of what it was under the Sandinistas and its economy has essentially been on hold since then, like a fly stuck in amber. Although numerous covert attempts have been made to remove Castro from power, his hold on the Cuban people is undeniably as firm as ever, and the boot of communism is firmly placed on their collective necks. Although Cuba ranks ahead of other countries in Latin America purely in average GDP, a third of the population live below the poverty line. Despite the promises of social change, and the availability of free health care and education, Cuba's economy continues to degrade even to this day. Although in the year 2000, public sector employment was 76% and private sector employment was 23% compared to the 1981 ratio of 91% to 8%, its annual GDP drops yearly. This is primarily due to the dwindling support from the former Soviet union. In the years 1990-1995, when subsidies substantially dried up, the national GDP dropped by more than 33%. The average wage at the end of 2005 was 334 regular pesos per month ($16.70 per month) and average monthly pension was $9, and Cuba must import over 80% of the food it rations to its population. Rationed food, rationed care and substandard living conditions are the price paid by their people for the redistribution of wealth and goods. It should also be noted that party leaders and Castro himself, do not have any rationing in their personal lives.

A further degradation of the Monroe Doctrine came in 1998 when America allowed the socialist forces under then career officer Hugo Chavez to seize power in an electioneering coup against the legitimate democratically elected government of President Carlos Perez in Venezuela after a failed military coup in 1992. Up until the rise of Chavez, Venezuela was a country that had been a free democracy since 1958. While Venezuela has not suffered as economically as Cuba, it has only been because of the enormous wealth of oil reserves at its disposal. The Venezuelan people still are not a free people, and it is one the prime sourcing grounds for drug trafficking into the United States. Crime rates are astonishingly high, and it is ranked as one of the most corrupt countries in the world by Transparency International in 2010.[107] The interesting point about the 1998 election in Venezuela is that it was electronically balloted and supposedly overseen by the Carter Center,[108] as well as other world organizations. Chavez promised social "change" to the Venezuelan people describing their goals as "laying the foundations of a new republic" to replace the existing one, which they cast as "party-dominated"--strikingly similar to previous leftist claims and also of the modern American Democrat party platform of 2008 that catapulted Barack Obama into office. Chávez'

---

[107] Since 1995, Transparency International (TI) has published an Annual Corruption Perceptions Index (CPI) ordering the countries of the world according to "the degree to which corruption is perceived to exist among public officials and politicians." The organization defines corruption as "the abuse of entrusted power for private gain."

[108] Founded by Jimmy Carter, The Carter Center works to advance human rights and alleviate human suffering. The Center is governed by a Board of Trustees, consisting of many prominent business persons, educators, former government officials, and eminent philanthropists.

promises of widespread social and economic reforms won the trust and favor of a primarily poor and working class following who felt betrayed by the Perez government that had grown fat from internal corruption. Chavez promoted the concept of "Rhine Capitalism"[109] (capitalism through planned economics), which was developed under Third Reich Germany; also known in many circles as fascism. It also reduces the value of the profit motive and replaces it with an honor based system[110]--all well and good if you are an humanitarian but it is a poor way to put food on the table.

As a result of Chavez' policies and economic engineering, Venezuela has one of the highest inflation rates in the world averaging 29.1% in 2010, and its economy is shrinking. It is expected to have shrunk by 2.9% in 2009 and further in 2010. A 2010 International Monetary Fund (IMF) study qualified as "delayed and weak" the economic recovery of Venezuela in comparison with other countries of the region that had emerged from the world economic crisis of 2008. According the Economist magazine, Venezuela also suffers from massive crime. In 2009 the homicide rate was approximately 57 per 100,000, one of the world's highest,

---

[109] Michel Albert first coined it in his book *Capitalisme contre Capitalisme*. It organizes economies under rules such as domination by the banks instead of the stock exchanges, close relationships between banks and companies well-adjusted balance of power between shareholders and managers, social partnership between employers and unions resulting in employees of higher loyalty, better educated employees thanks to something like the dual education system ,more regulated markets and, last but most importantly, shared values by most of the citizens regarding the ideas of equality and solidarity.

[110] In the Rhine model a long tradition frees the members of a profession (e.g. doctors and lawyers) from the need to chase profit in order to be able to concentrate in a disinterested fashion on serving the public good. The service is a kind of an honor, and the expression for the payment in these areas (*Honorar*) is closely related to this underlying idea.

having trebled in the previous decade. Human rights abuses are rampant as well, critics of the leftist government are often imprisoned and there is no judicial watch. According to a Human Rights Watch 2011 report:

> Supreme Court President Luisa Estella Morales held that laws in Venezuela 'respond to an ideological purpose.' The keynote speaker during the public event, Justice Fernando Torre Alba, stated that the judiciary 'has the duty to participate in the effective implementation... of the government's public policy to develop... a Bolivarian and democratic socialism' and that all courts, including the Supreme Court, 'must severely ... sanction behaviors or cases that undermine the construction of [such] socialism.' (Universal Periodic Review of Venezuela, Human Rights Watch, 2011)

Had America enforced its Monroe Doctrine in Venezuela, as it had in other Latin American nations previously, Chavez would still be in prison there, and the Venezuelan people most likely would be living in a freer society. Although such interfering behavior is condemned by America's critics, most often leftist critics, the end result of a more productive and free society outweighs the concerns of possible corruption and American influence. Instead America chose to stand by and allow fascism to take hold in Venezuela, and allowed a future Hitler to grow unchecked only 2000 nautical miles from the Texas border. Worse, its massive crude oil reserves are being plundered to enrich our enemies rather than the Venezuelan people.

The horrors of state sponsored crime against its own people, communism and the mass poverty it brings, has largely been avoided in Nicaragua, Panama and Costa Rica where American presidents have taken an active role in protecting democracy from leftism and communism. Today Nicaragua supplies the US with imports such as high quality rum, tobacco and beef, and its people live under a freely elected government defeating the Sandinista communist party several times in recent elections. While Nicaragua's economy is still recovering from the Sandinista insurgency and the US embargoes of the mid-1980's it is currently voted the second best place to start a new business in all the Latin American nations and is considered one of the freest economies in the world. It is growing in leaps and bounds even without the massive wealth of oil exports.

Costa Rica and Panama also enjoy unusual freedom and prosperity compared to Venezuela's and Cuba's socialistic and leftist policies. Costa Rica is also a significant member of the United Nations and has been on the U.N. Security Council several times. Its literacy rate is the highest of all the Central American nations. Costa Rica also developed along the American lines of economic gain with its people being forced to develop their own lands much as our settlers did in the American Midwest of the same period. Since there was a considerable lack of indigenous people to enslave or use as forced labor, they became a highly self-sufficient and independent people. The Costa Ricans developed a reputation for egalitarianism, hard work ethics and a largely peaceful development compared to their Latin American neighbors.

This is further evidence that a largely self-sufficient people tend to develop faster and more prosperously than more socialized countries.

The Monroe Doctrine in the Americas took on a new role under President George W. Bush with the attacks on New York City and Washington D.C. in September of 2001. His interpretation of American foreign policy to include the defense of American lands and waters under the concept of a first strike came to be known as the Bush Doctrine.[111] This extension of Monroe's theories held that America had the moral and legal right to militarily attack any nation which America perceived as a direct threat to the safety of the American people. Up until this change in American policy, the United States had never launched an attack against a sovereign nation except in self-defense. Bush extended this theory to include the possibility of a pre-emptive strike as an act of self-defense, which was a highly controversial interpretation of America's foreign policy. The theory was that since foreign powers now had the ability to strike at the United States with weapons of "mass destruction" and do so from the relative safety of their own nations without regard to distance, the United States had the moral right to remove that threat.

---

[111] The Bush Doctrine is a phrase used to describe various related foreign policy principles of former United States president George W. Bush. The phrase was first used by Charles Krauthammer in June 2001 to describe the Bush Administration's unilateral withdrawals from the Anti-Ballistic Missile Treaty and the Kyoto Protocol. The phrase initially described the policy that the United States had the right to secure itself against countries that harbor or give aid to terrorist groups, which was used to justify the 2001 invasion of Afghanistan.

The Bush Doctrine may have led to two highly unpopular wars, one in Iraq and one in Afghanistan, but ultimately the world may have been significantly safer, if not for America, then certainly for the Iraqi people[112] much as the Monroe Doctrine did for the peoples of South America. Despite accusations that the invasion of the nation of Iraq was for oil, the Iraqi people have still maintained ownership of its considerable oil reserves and its democratically elected people (a first in the region) will be able to administer that wealth for its own people, rather than for the personal gain of a dictator. The days of a brutal dictator murdering children in front of their parents as punishment for perceived slights is now over in Iraq. It still remains for history to determine if America's moves in these two nations improved the lives of their citizens, but if history is any indication of the future, things bode well for the Iraqi people, much as it did for the free nations of South America.

Time will tell. This is assuming of course, our failures in the Gulf in a post Bush era, and post Monroe doctrine era, do not come back to haunt us as the Middle East slips into anarchy under the watch of Progressive President Obama.

---

[112] On June 30 and December 11, 2009, the Iraqi ministry of oil awarded service contracts to international oil companies for some of Iraq's many oil fields. Oil fields contracted include the "super-giant" Majnoon Field, Halfaya Field, West Qurna Field and Rumaila Field. In February 2011, Citigroup included Iraq in a group of countries which it described as a "Global Growth Generator," that it argued will enjoy significant economic growth in the future.

11 THE AMERICAN WAY IN ASIA

History proves that all dictatorships, all authoritarian forms of government are transient. Only democratic systems are not transient. Whatever the shortcomings, mankind has not devised anything superior. – Vladimir Putin

What is being asked of America now is to follow the more traditional paths of greatness that other nations have followed, a tradition of communal and shared economic and intellectual theory. Other nations for generations have held their philosophical ground that a planned and controlled population is a more productive one. In fact, as democracy has increased around the world, so has the power of government and its controls on their native economies. While many hold that democracy is the wave of the future, America still stands alone in its unbridled economic theories and its bold and forward thinking political theory. Most nations still have not been able to close the gap with America in either its military and political influence nor in its economic growth on a per capita basis. This is because while more nations than ever before are democracies they are democracies *in name only* without the protections in place such as the American Constitution, and their economies are still largely planned by government and its bureaucracies. Brazil is a democracy for example, yet with its communist president and election process it could hardly be called free—its people are at the whim and mercy of its government.

Many point to the recent success of China in the areas of manufacturing and economic expansion. The Chinese economy has been primarily controlled from its Central Committee and is considered still a Communist country. But how did it achieve its success? Certainly not through Communism but rather through a surprisingly free hand in open capitalistic development. In fact you can track Chinese success almost to the moment when it took over Hong Kong from the British in 1997.

Hong Kong was under British dominion until July 1, 1997 by a consensual treaty established 100 years earlier and ended British rule after 157 years of control. Simultaneously with the turnover of Hong Kong to China, just two years later in 1999, the Portuguese island nation of Macau was turned over to them as well. If you look at the Chinese GDP from the period of 1997 to 2007 you will find that the Chinese GDP went from about 900 billion dollars to an astronomical 5 trillion dollars in 2009, with over a trillion dollars of this annual growth increase during one of the worst global recessions ever faced.

The evidence of how that happened is directly related to the takeover of those two small colonies. In 1997 in order to ease fears that China was going to convert Hong Kong into another poor province of the communists, the 15th National Communist Party Congress met in September. Then President Jiang Zemin announced plans to sell, merge or close the vast majority of State Owned Enterprises (SOE's) in his call for increased "non-public ownership." This was done in order that the Hong Kong economy could merge seamlessly into the Chinese economy. Even more astounding, by the March 1998 session of the 9th National People's Congress it had endorsed the idea of the privatization of Chinese industries that was previously controlled directly by the Party. By 2000, China claimed success in its three year effort to make the majority of large SOE's profitable--and in doing so transferred most of these SOE's into private hands. Although these companies were still under the influence of the Chinese government, they operated with a level of freedom that is rarely seen even in American private industry today. In fact, Chinese companies are subject to less government regulation and a lower tax base than most of their American counterparts—even if they potentially could be seized and controlled by the state.

The Chinese saw the value of free enterprise, and simply incorporated the American business model of the 1950's into a communist empire. They did not import the business model of 1999 American business but 1959, with few environmental protections and wide open capitalistic practices. As of 2010 the Chinese economy, which for over 100 years barely hovered above the level of a third world country, is the second largest economy in the world and is poised to eclipse the American GDP by sometime in 2013.

It was the beacon of American free enterprise—The American Way--that built the Chinese economy, not the planned economies of Eastern Europe and South America. China's growth was its unbridled plumbing of its own energy reserves. In 2003 China embarked on a massive expansion of its energy industry, similar in scope to the industrialization age of America in the 1900's. China poured large amounts of capital into their domestic oil and coal industries while simultaneously decreasing the regulatory powers of oversight committees. Regulatory powers of the central bureaucracy were decentralized into local provinces. This move to the local level, rather than the federalized approach, is opposite of the path that America is moving towards. The decentralization of an nation's economy has untold economic benefits, as China is discovering, largely through the elimination of corruption and power.[113] In short, they allowed their 'states' to control commerce and enterprise rather than a federal or centralized oversight.

---

[113] Decentralization is the process of dispersing decision-making governance closer to the people and/or citizens. It includes the dispersal of administration or governance in sectors or areas like engineering, management science, political science, politica economy, sociology and economics. Decentralization is also possible in the dispersal of population and employment.

China's energy industry is highly competitive with no single company allowed to dominate its marketplaces. The modern concept of American "utilities" is largely unheard of in China as companies are encouraged to compete in decentralized markets on a per province basis through deregulation and tax breaks. Market factors now determine energy prices, rather than government panels, and fierce competition has allowed energy prices to drop and the blooming reserves and stockpiles of energy are exported worldwide. Although China is still dependent on foreign oil imports, it is mainly due to explosive economic growth, not its own internal controls.[114] America's modern development of government controlled utilities and price setting by committee has only raised and exacerbated both our energy costs and slow development as opposed to the now Chinese model of energy development.

When you examine the worldwide economic patterns that have emerged in the past five years, the most successful economic models rely heavily on working their own vast national energy and resource reserves rather than conservation "green" methods and dependency on foreign imports. China, Russia and other nations that are growing are exporters and energy powerhouses, not importers and conservationists.[115] As a percentage of their total energy

---

[114] Justin Yifu Lin the chief of the China Centre for Economic Research at Beijing University claims that China uses 15% of the world's energy. Sinopec is China's largest producer and supplier of oil and petrochemical products and China's second largest producer of crude oil. PetroChina supplies the country with natural gas and oil and according to the Forbes ranking is the largest publicly owned company in China.-Chinaorbit.com

[115] Russia exports 70% of oil produced, about 7 million of 10.12 million barrels a day

consumption, both China and Russia use far more of their own energy reserves than imported products.

Russia has followed the model of Chinese decentralization and has also seen enormous growth in the past 10 years. Although it too has seen a drop in the global recession of 2007-2011, it still is growing faster than the US GDP--almost 4.1% in 2010. If the US economy was growing at that rate, most of its economic woes would be irrelevant. More importantly, Russia is using its new energy economic clout to generate substantial revenues for its government[116]-- revenues being used to develop its weak economy and expand its already considerable military strength.[117]

Although Russia suffered a setback in 2008-2009, as most nations did, it has largely avoided the economic flattening the US has suffered. Like China, it has followed the economic model of American industry in the 1950's involving decentralization and a lax regulatory environment. President Putin has remolded the Russian economy as an economic engine through decentralization into local hands, and allowed private industry to expand its influence through privatization.

(2010), the largest net oil export of any country, as well as a major supply to the European Union The entire Middle East, in comparison, exports 20 million barrels daily.

[116] On July 2008 Russia's president signed a law allowing the government to allocate strategic oil and gas deposits on the continental shelf without an auction procedure. On February 17, 2011, Russia signed a deal with China, stating that in return for $25 billion in Chinese loans to Russian oil companies, Russia will supply China with large quantities of crude oil via new pipelines for the next 20 years

[117] More money is arriving both for personnel and equipment, and Russian Prime Minister Vladimir Putin said in June 2008 that monetary allowances for servicemen in permanent-readiness units will be raised significantly. Funding for new equipment has greatly risen in recent years, and the Russian defense industry continues to develop new weapons systems for the Ground Forces.

During Putin's eight years in office, industry grew by 75%, investments increased by 125% and agricultural production and construction increased as well. Real incomes more than doubled and the average monthly salary increased eightfold from $80 to $640. The volume of consumer credit between 2000–2006 increased 45 times, and during that same time period the middle class grew from eight million to 55 million, an increase of nearly seven times. The number of people living below the poverty line also decreased from 30% in 2000 to 14% in 2008. As of 2011, according to US Department of Labor statistics, nearly 50 million people in the US now qualify and receive food stamps, which require a person to be below the poverty line, a number that is nearly 18%, higher than the supposedly poverty stricken former Soviet Union. All of this and more is due to the development of industry along capitalistic lines—not socialistic or communist ones.

It is clear that the "Americanization" of the formerly planned economies of China and Russia have had nearly the same results on their economies as it did on the American economy of our earlier industrialization periods. While these nations are hardly "free" nations, as they have moved more toward the model of America they have succeeded, while America, with its move toward more regulation and a planned economy has floundered. Countries like Germany, France, Greece, Italy and England are still drowning in their own government controlled economic planning and have not had any significant GDP growth. The United Kingdom's GDP in 2000 was barely a trickle above 1.5 trillion, and 11 years later it has had only marginal growth coming in at 2.1 trillion. The

Greek economy has had almost zero growth during this period, and Italy's growth has moved only about 500 billion in over 10 years.

In the United States our GDP growth has almost been linearly upwards until approximately 2006 when the Progressive laden Democrat party took over complete control of the American economy through Congress. The 2006 House, in lock step with the Democratic Senate under the direction Nancy Pelosi, issued more new economic regulatory committees, new laws, and new oversight rules in two years than in the past 50 years of US economic history. In 2002, under the direction of the Tom Daschle (D-SD) led Senate, the Sarbanes-Oxley Act was the largest single bill regarding economic oversight in American history and was passed and signed into law in response to a financial crisis that shook markets due largely to misreporting of inherent values of companies to reporting agencies.

Written by US Senator Paul Sarbanes (D-MD) and US Representative Michael G. Oxley (R-OH), President George W. Bush signed it into law, stating it included "the most far-reaching reforms of American business practices since the time of Franklin D. Roosevelt."[118] In the years of 2001 to 2008, the Congress was almost entirely dominated by Democrat economic theory, and government expanded to ridiculous levels. Adding to the fracas was the attack in 2001 which led President Bush to create an entirely new government bureau,

---

[118] Bumiller, Elisabeth (2002-07-31). "Bush Signs Bill Aimed at Fraud in Corporations". The New York Times.

the Department of Homeland Security, which consumes large amounts of tax dollars annually--as much as 60 billion dollars a year in 2010.

Government size and scope expanded more in this period than in any previous period in United States history, even greater than that during World War II. In 2000 government spending had not yet reached 1.8 trillion dollars annually. By 2011 that number has swollen to almost 4.8 trillion. This represents over a 200% increase in less than a decade, consuming almost the entire GDP of the United States in a single year. A government for the people now had become a people for the government. Naturally when economic markets began to collapse in 2008, government revenues slipped as well, but spending had not. As a result, deficits soared, and America began to resemble the economies of the European nations they had fled 200 years earlier.

When the financial markets began to collapse again in 2007-2008 under the direction of a new Pelosi-Reid Democratic led Congress and the failures of the markets to control Fannie Mae's and Freddie Mac's excessive social agenda lending practices,[119] a rescue of the industry became almost impossible under traditional means. Many critics blamed Sarbanes–Oxley for the low number of Initial Public Offerings (IPO's) on the American stock exchanges during 2008. In November 2008 Newt Gingrich and co-author David W. Kralik called on Congress to repeal Sarbanes–Oxley in

---

[119] Gregg: Congress' Social Agenda Caused Financial Crisis Monday, April 4, 2011 By Dan Weil

order to allow more IPO's to inflate the market back up to normal levels to allow normal market forces to correct the impending collapse. They were largely ignored and capital dried up for American business to use for its recovery and the die was set as America slipped deeper into recession, thus ensuring Obama's election. Business ran to government for aid and relied on TARP funds to avoid total collapse, rather than simply borrowing and leveraging the now poisoned real estate markets. Worse, the original TARP bailout fund of 180 billion as suggested by President Bush, was inflated to 787 billion by now President Obama, is an effort to "stimulate" the American economy into recovery. This economic plan, a natural ideological extension of Roosevelt's New Deal, had the same effect on the American economy in 2009 as it did in 1932--an overall flattening of the markets and joblessness rising to double digit levels.

As America shifted toward government reliance it too began to suffer the ennui of a European style economy. Stagnant growth, high unemployment and rampant apathy of business to expand and innovate, which was always the standard bearer of American ingenuity, now had become the norm. The relationship between Chinese and Russian success and open markets, and America's failures under closing its markets is definitive and undeniable.

America was now a nation enslaved to its economic masters, much as it was in pre-Revolutionary times, and in the pre-Civil War slave and sharecropper South. It also had the same response from its workers, a general apathy and malaise settling in on the American worker as they gave up on the

American dream and settled instead for the new Obama led American way of life—dependency and a reliance on government.

12 AND IN THE END

Our greatest happiness does not depend on the condition of life in which chance has placed us, but is always the result of a good conscience, good health, occupation, and freedom in all just pursuits. -- Thomas Jefferson

Considering the enormous contributions America has made to the world community one would think that the American style of doing things and accomplishing goals would be the model of the world. Unfortunately, it isn't. Only the nations that have understood the value of American capitalism and free enterprise have moved forward in the modern world. Those that have not continue to be racked with debt and economic malaise. Our former enemies of China and Russia have learned from our failures and our successes. Economically beaten by 1985, they have simply copied our pattern of success and encouraged America to wallow in the misery they designed in failure 50 years previously.

The world, despite its considered move toward democracy, is not much different in its organization from that of 200 years ago. European style democracies are still subject to the idiosyncrasies of their elected leaders who wield far more power than is either good for their country or their respective democracies. Other "second world" nations such as Russia, Brazil and other former communist and dictatorial nations are democracies in name only. They carry the banner called democracy but are really just feudalistic systems where a few call the shots for many. Monarchies are still very real threats to human rights and freedom in many nations including several Middle East nations. Even England's aristocratic monarchy is making moves to keep the people less free despite its Parliamentary protections.

It is America, and the American Way, that stands alone in its definitive list of Constitutional rights. America enjoys liberties and protections unheard of in most nations, such as the freedom of the press, the right to own a gun and its equal protections under the law. While separate and definitive classes of wealth exist in American culture, even the poorest of Americans live better than 90% of the wealthiest non-Americans. The modern day Progressives of the Democratic party are still stymied daily by the inherent protections of the American Constitution even though it had been written 200 years earlier by men that could not of conceived of notions such as socialism, communism or men like Barack Obama whose hucksterism would sell them to the nation.

Americans enjoy unappreciated comforts of equal access to quality housing, sanitation and food that cannot be rivaled anywhere in the world. These comforts were not derived from the development of government but rather the development of a free economy. While corruption exists, it is not institutionalized as it is in many other nations, and when discovered it is aggressively prosecuted and punished. The American justice system, while being called unfair in some circles has an astounding record of civility both in its application and punishment particularly when compared with the stark and harsh prison sentences in most third world nations. A sentence in an American prison of 8 or 10 years is hardly the death sentence it is in a prison in Chile or Libya.

The main reasons for this are varied, but it essentially boils down to two factors, ignorance and jealousy. Americans are widely ignorant of the horrific and unsanitary conditions that most of the world lives under, and non-Americans who may be aware of this significant disparity feel that it came at the expense of their own existence. The evidence in this book suggests otherwise, but nevertheless this feeling pervades other cultures, particularly in cultures where this disparity is the widest, such as in Middle Eastern third world nations like Iran, Afghanistan and Libya. These nations' peoples have only limited access to Westernized ideas, culture and wealth and their understanding of American culture is informed by what is told to them by their governments who have much to gain by their continued ignorance.

America is a popular enemy of most oppressive regimes. The more oppressive the culture, the more hostile it is to American ideas, culture and prosperity. They attempt to spread that hostility by infiltrating the cultures in between America and their own. By insinuating their own evil into cultures less prepared and less disparate than their own they hope to mold the world more to their own ideals and thus isolate American liberty and freedom as an enemy of the whole rather than their own limited ideas. By making a European nation more oppressive either through legal or illegal means, it widens the gulf between the world and America. Eventually that gulf will become so great American theories will be viewed as extreme and an anomaly rather than the other way around. The persons and leaders that perpetrate the myths of American racism, violence and imperialism seek to turn the tables of popular opinion against America.

Americans cannot allow this happen. To do so would let the fruits of a free economy and liberty to simply blacken the fields of freedom, and let them fall fallow. Freedom must be carefully protected at all times. It is essential that Americans not allow themselves to fall under the spell of viewing their own nation as something to be derided, despised and changed. The old arguments of "Fifth Columnists" is not a figure of speech nor an illusory threat but one of real significance and danger. The walls of a well-defended castle are rarely broken down by the direct fire of cannonades but rather by the unseen threat of sappers and starvation by siege. This is what is happening to America now, and much of it is at the hands of well-meaning Americans who simply want to be more like the rest of the world in the interest of fairness. While a noble ideal, doing so ultimately is counterproductive to the intent, which is a safer and saner world.

The greatest danger of being willing participants to the tragedy occurring in America is that America's ultimate failure will come at the hands of good people who have been misled into doing a great evil. It is easy to believe that a reliance on government programs and social plans will solve the problems of society such as poverty, drug abuse and crime. Above all else, Americans believe that no matter their own background we are all the same, and all men are equal. It is easy to believe that the poor man in the street is there by bad luck or by the hands of a criminal act rather than by his own poor life choices. Americans want to correct the issue of bad luck or bad decisions through the entitlements of government which in a capitalistic society should be less plentiful and widespread, instead of encouraging and developing free enterprise.

But by doing so, by allowing government to expand its influence in the interest of helping fellow man and positioning America as a poor cousin to a European style of governance, we move away from the very thing that protects our fellow man from oppression. By moving away from the historically important value system of self-reliance and independence we in turn exchange one problem for another problem--that of an expansive and socially controlling government that now not only provides a basket of food for the hungry but tells us how to eat that basket and takes the basket from those that plucked the fruit in the first place. These are not the values of the America that made us great. It is the values of other countries which have failed to provide the same level of wealth and freedom that capitalism and democracy have provided us.

We cannot provide for others when they cannot provide for themselves. We must lead the way for others to follow in that path. Americans must also come to the inescapable truth that many take for granted, that freedom has a down side as well as an upside. It means that you are free to make a bad choice as well as a good one--otherwise it is not a free choice at all.

Americans have come to see leadership as braggadocio. They have been taught in schools that the profit motive of capitalism equates to greed. We are now teaching our children the false tenet that the concept of government creating grand projects such as the Panama Canal and the Highway System is the same as fulfilling basic needs of clothing, housing and food. That the streets are filled with racial prejudices that preclude minorities from making it on their own. That the very air we breathe and the paths that we take are the jurisdiction of government rather than of God. This is a very great threat to the American way of life, whether it was intended or not.

America was and is a nation by the people and for the people. Superman is revoking his citizenship sought to protect and insulate America from the backlash over his bold actions, but in doing so denied to the world that this is the very definition of what America is all about and the very reason why it is great. His shame and fear of the downside of his actions is what leftists are trying to teach Americans now—that success is merely at the expense of others.

This is what America must seek to avoid. Americans must express pride in our great nation, not in spite of its differences from other nations, but rather because of it. We must not be ashamed to be successful, wealthy or powerful.

Neither dictators, nor tyrants, nor the brutal indifference of bureaucracy must be allowed to replace it.

The American Way: Why Superman Got It Wrong

ABOUT THE AUTHOR

ABOUT THE AUTHOR

Tom was born in Yonkers, NY and in 1968 was the youngest member of Mensa in the country at that time and is to date, the highest tested individual in Mensa at that age. Educated at the University of California, Tom moved to Arizona after college in 1994 and went into the insurance business. After being a top agent for NY Life Insurance, he decided to become an independent broker in 2005 (Lotusbenefits.com) and is now a successful entrepreneur and author of the column "Conservative Issues from the Desert." He calls Surprise, AZ his home, where he does volunteer work for various issues around the state. Conservative, funny and a candidly frank speaker, Tom is available for consultation and speaking engagements on subjects from politics to marketing. "The Return of the Kings" his first book, spent two weeks on the Amazon best seller list nationwide. His most recent work is "The American Way: Why Superman Got It Wrong".

You can read more of his musings and articles at www.thomas-purcell.com, as well as excerpts from his books, where he welcomes comments, discussion and offers free subscriptions.

www.ingramcontent.com/pod-product-compliance
Lightning Source LLC
Chambersburg PA
CBHW060253290526
45789CB00001B/315